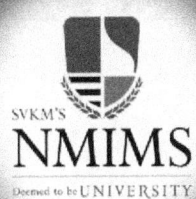

NMIMS Management Review

● ISSN: 0971-1023 ● Volume: XXIX ● Issue: 2 ● April-June 2021

Editorial
The New Beginning
Pp(i-iii)

Radhika Thanki & D.M Pestonjee
Role Stress, Psychological Well Being and Resilience among Working Professionals
Pp(1-15)

K. Ramya & Bhuvaneshwari D.
Dynamic Interaction between NIFTY 50 and Nifty Sectoral Indices: An Empirical Study on Indian Stock Indices
Pp(16-23)

Shaunak Roy & Shivaji Banerjee
Cross-Cultural Dissimilarities in the Perception of Brand Personality of Select Smartphones: Evidence from West Bengal, India and Bangladesh
Pp(24-50)

Aparna Bhatia & Megha Mahendru
Cost Efficiency Vis-à-Vis Revenue Efficiency Analysis of Indian Scheduled Commercial Banks in a Dynamic Environment
Pp(51-71)

NMIMS Management Review

Volume XXIX   Issue 2   April-June 2021

Editor in Chief
Dr. Tapan Kumar Panda

Managing Editor
Dr. Mayank Joshipura

Editorial Board

- Dr. Amandeep Dhir
  University of Agder, Kristiansand, Norway

- Dr. Anil Mishra
  Western Sydney University, Australia.

- Dr. Elizabeth Rose
  Leeds University Business School, UK.

- Dr. Gregory Prastacos
  Stevens Institute of Technology, USA

- Dr. Jatin Pancholi
  Southhampton University, UK.

- Dr. Jose Arturo Garza-Reyes
  University of Derby, UK

- Dr. Rita Biswas
  Albany State University, NewYork, USA

- Dr. Stephen Goodwin
  Illinois State University, USA

- Dr. Sumit Kundu
  Florida International University, USA

- Dr. Sunil Sahadev
  University of Brighton, UK.

- Dr. S N Rao
  Shailesh J. Mehta School of Management
  IIT Bombay, India

- Dr. Tarun Sen
  Virginia Tech, USA

Advisory Board

Dr. Arun Sharma

Dr. Anupam Rastogi

Dr. Chandrima Sikdar

Dr. Meena Galliara

Prof. Papiya De

Dr. Ranjan Chakravarty

Dr. Somnath Roy

Dr. Veena Vohra

Published by :  **Black Eagle Books**
USA address: 7464 Wisdom Lane, Dublin, OH 43016
E-mail: info@blackeaglebooks.org   Website: www.blackeaglebooks.org

ISBN: 978-1-64560-194-4
Library of Congress Control Number: 2021940935

Copyright (C) 2021 by NMIMS - Deemed to be University,   All rights reserved.

No part of this publication may be reproduced, stored in a retrieval system, or transmitted in any form or by any means, electronic, mechanical, photocopying, recording, scanning, or otherwise, except as permitted under Section 107 or 108 of the 1976 United States Copyright Act, without either the prior written permission of the Editor. Requests to the Editor for permission should be addressed to the - Managingeditor@nmims.edu

Web address.: https://management-review.nmims.edu

Editorial

A New Beginning

Covid- 2019 has brought in unparalleled challenges to human civilization. We have faced such situations in the long past and assumed that the development in science and technology has insulated us from such dreaded pandemics. Though we had few similar incidents like AIDS, SARS, and Ebola virus had geographic limitations with no such high impact and global effect as the current problem. This pandemic has challenged the existence and growth of nations bringing in problems that have both short- term as well as very long- term impacts.

The human race is peculiar in nature. We are neither stronger, faster, bigger nor the most prudent ones (some say honey bees and penguins are more intelligent than us) but we have these uncanny abilities to survive against all adversaries and bounce back to normalcy. Resilience is the key to human survival and growth. Research on resilience in psychology has confined itself to a uni-dimensional approach and work context only. It is time to research more on a social or national level. Resilience is an important behavior for success, growth, and survival (King, Newman &Luthans, 2016) for organizations and people working in it. Now we need to refocus on nations, societies, races, and cultures to answer the question- why some of these institutions cope better; bounce back faster than others. Some scholars look at resilience as a dynamic process while others sees it as a trait (King et al, 2016).However, all definitions describe resilience as the ability to deal with and adapt to adversities.

Recent researches have highlighted the psychological capital concept and how the same can be built and maintained in personal resilience (Linnenluecke, 2017). Individuals at work place and society experience sudden collapse due to physical fatigue and adverse phenomena (like Covid-19) respectively. The coping mechanism in a societal context goes beyond psychological traits/assets and brings in larger, complex issues.

While we open up our societies, workplaces and businesses in a post Covid-19 world, we are likely to face a multitude of problems in coping with the adverse effects of the pandemic at individual, organizational, and national level. Physical health, as well as the psychological health of people will play a crucial role in workplace health and performance. There is a need to relook at health holistically as a combination of the human body and mind and how they interact with each other. The bio-psychological and bio- physiological aspects of a person's functioning need further study to understand resilience at a wider social context (Rook Caroline et al, 2018).

There is abundance of literature on integrative approach to resilience in health psychology literature. Resilience is an outcome of successful adaptation to adversity and that more resilient individuals demonstrate a greater capacity to quickly regain equilibrium physiologically, psychologically, and in social relations following stressful events (Zautra, Hall and Murray, 2008, p.42).

Workplace resilience may not be as linear as it seems as stressful events may occur randomly over a prolonged period. We have this understanding that when physical systems are stressed beyond a certain tolerance level, adaptive mechanisms carry the risk of being dysfunctional leading to dis-regulation and low grade mal-adaptation. The recent lockdown and physical confinement of individuals might have carried similar mal-adaptation. The inability to maintain homeostasis has the potential to lead to a short-term as well long-term recovery process. (Halson et al 2003; Shepard, 2001; Smith 2003).This is posing a challenge to therapists and opportunitiesfor behavioral scientists to explore in a post-Covid-19 world.

The researchers need to take a cross-disciplinary view on 'resilience' as an interesting phenomenon in the new world. The exploration should be done holistically by connecting researchers from different sciences. Meaningful research is to be done to identify key components of resilience at individual and society at large; to understand the mechanism of how resilience is created andhow it leads to improved health and job performance. The health psychology perspective will have a meaningful bearing on 'resilience research' as resilience is a process of coping with disruptive, stressful, or challenging life events in a way that provides the individual with additional protective and coping skills than prior to the disruption that results from the event (Richardson, Neiger, Jensen and Kumfer, 1990).

Earlier studies have also identified that cardiovascular responses have interaction with behavioral change and coping behavior (Orbrist, 1976). He also suggested that coping behavior had an association with the situation. This will help in building newer coping skills and helping people to overcome stress from the catastrophic impact of Covid-19. People need to develop faster and accurate coping skills and get trained on the same so that overall the society can return to normalcy (Blascovich& Mendes, 2000).

The recent sudden spurt of Covid cases has put lots of stress on health care workers. If a researcher is looking for a domain to do resilience research, the healthcare industry is a good fertile ground. Resilience involves the interaction between three factors: the stressor, the context, and personal characteristics (McAllister and McKinnon, 2009). The stressors come from the environment- fast- paced, changing, uncertain, high workload plus the emotional labour of patient care (Scammell, 2017). The way the individual responds to these can be positively influenced by increasing understanding of the context of care and how one responds to it. Jackson et al (2007) identified several strategies to support the development of resilience among health workers that includes building positive professional relationships; increasing insight into one's stress triggers, and self-protective mechanisms. Focusing on health care workers will be a good idea to study resilience in a post Covid world.

Now let's talk about NMIMS Management Review- our journal. There has been a smooth editorial transition to the journal. The earlier team of Editor in Chief and Managing Editor have successfully completed their tenure and have paved the way for me and Prof MayankJoshipura who has a big role to play as Managing Editor. We also have got a new international editorial board in place now to guide the journal to a greater height. The journal has its own heritage as we present Volume- 29, Issue -2 to you. I hope the journal will travel miles now as we are getting top- notch papers these days. Both the number and quality of papers are posing a daunting challenge to quickly turn around the research papers. I have set a new process that is quite an author engaging and we will continue to communicate with you at every stage of the progress of a paper so that all the three stakeholders' i.e. editorial team, author, and reviewers have enough breathing time to work on the papers.

I am happy that we will have print versions available now in Order to Print (OTP) format on Amazon. So authors can order print versions of the journal directly from Amazon. The new international publishing partner will be publishing the journal from Ohio, USA. The journal will have a global reach. I intend to take the journal currently from WOS to a Scopus indexed and ABDC ranked journal in near future, but all three stakeholders play crucial roles for the success of NMIMS Management Review. Please do write to me if you wish to contribute as an author/ reviewer.

My idea of writing this note on 'resilience' is to prioritize the challenges we are going to face in a post Covid world and also give a cue to researchers to focus when human civilization is reconciling back to normalcy. Please do write to me your views about the papers, journal, and any other key input that will make our journal far reaching, significant, and impactful in the domain of management and business research.

Dr Tapan K Panda
Editor in Chief (EIC)
NMIMS Management Review
Email: tapankumar.panda@nmims.edu

References:

Blascovich, J., & Mendes, W. B. (2000). Challenge and Threat Appraisals: The Role of Affective Cues. In J. P. Forgas (Ed.), Feeling and Thinking: The Role of Affect in Social Cognition (pp. 59-82). Cambridge, England: Cambridge University Press.

Halson, S., Lancaster, G., Jeukendrup, A., & Gleeson, M. (2003).Immunological Responses to Overreaching in Cyclists. Medicine and Science in Sports and Exercise, 35(5), 854-861. doi: 10.1249/01.MSS.0000064964.80040.E9

Jackson, D., Firtko, A., &Edenborough, M. (2007). Personal Resilience as a Strategy for Surviving and Thriving in the Face of Workplace Adversity: A Literature Review. Journal of Advanced Nursing, 60, 1-9. doi: 10.1111/j.1365- 2648.2007.04412.x

King, D. D., Newman, A., &Luthans, F. (2016). Not if, but When We Need Resilience in the Workplace. Journal of Organizational Behaviour, 37, 782-786. doi: 10.1002/job.2063

Linnenluecke, M. K. (2017). Resilience in Business and Management Research: A Review of Influential Publications and a Research Agenda. International Journal of Management Reviews, 19, 4-30. doi: 10.1111/ijmr.12076

McAllister M, McKinnon J. The Importance of Teaching and Learning Resilience in the Health Disciplines: A Critical Review of the Literature. Nurse Education Today. 2009; 29(4): 371-379.

Orbrist, P. A. (1976). The Cardiovascular BehaviouralInteraction—As it appears Today. Psychophysiology, 13(2), 95-107. doi:10.1111/j.1469- 8986.1976.tb00081

Richardson, G. E., Neiger, B. L., Jensen, S., &Kumpfer, K. L. (1990). The Resiliency Model, Health Education, 21(6), 33-39. doi: 10.1080/00970050.1990.10614589

Rook, Caroline, Lee Smith, James Johnstone, Claire Rossato, Guillermo Felipe Lpez Sanchez, Arturo Diaz Suarez and Justin Roberts (2018), Reconceptualising Workplace Resilience – A Cross Disciplinary Perspective, Anales de Psicologica, 34,2, 2018

Scammell Janet (2017), Resilience in the Workplace: Personal and Organizational Factors, British Journal of Nursing, 26, 16.

Shephard, R. (2001). Chronic Fatigue Syndrome: An update. Sports Medicine, 31(3), 167-194. doi: 10.2165/00007256-200131030-00003

Smith, L. (2003). Overtraining, excessive exercise and altered immunity- Is this a T Helper-1 versus T Helper-2 lymphocyte response? Sports Medicine, 33(5), 347-364. doi: 10.2165/00007256-200333050-00002

Zautra, A., Hall, J., & Murray, K. (2008). Resilience: a new integrative approach to health and mental health research. Health Psychology Review, 2(1), 41-64. doi: 10.1080/17437190802298568

Role Stress, Psychological Well Being and Resilience among Working Professionals

Radhika Thanki
PhD Scholar, School of Petroleum Management
Pandit Deendayal Energy University, Gandhinagar
D. M. Pestonjee
GSPL Chair Professor, School of Petroleum Management,
Pandit Deendayal Energy University, Gandhinagar

Received 3 February 2020
Revised 8 March 2020
Accepted 12 February 2021

Abstract

External demand on biological, social and psychological equilibrium of individuals, called as stress, has adverse impact on health, performance and wellbeing of an individual. One of the principal sectors of life, job and organization, leads to workplace stress. In both developed and developing nations job stress poses significant health risk to employees leading to anxiety, burnout, cardiovascular disease, depression, and insomnia. Declared as worldwide epidemic by WHO, stress, not only results in large emotional cost to worker's performance and financial burden on organization but also accounts for accidents at workplace.

In the context of this study, the factor of psychological well-being is a state of mind which includes an individual's desire to live life joyfully, and attain equilibrium between activities at work and efforts to build psychological resilience where resilience is the ability to bounce back or rebound from difficulty or misfortune or even increased responsibility.

This analysis which establishes quantitative relationship among organization role stress, psychological well-being and resilience at work can be used by organizations and academia in order to gain insights into organizations role stress, psychological well-being and resilience at workplace.

Keywords : Role Stress, Psychological Well-being, Resilience, Occupational Stress

Introduction

A healthy work place is one where the pressures are in harmony with the capabilities and resources of an employee, with the extent of control employees have over their work, and with the care they receive from those who matter the most in the organization. However, the present human condition prevailing at workplace unfortunately comprises of stress along with other mental health issues. Pressure perceived as tolerable by an employee, may keep him/her attentive, driven, able to work and learn, based on the available resources and individual characteristics. However, when that pressure becomes intolerable or unmanageable it leads to stress.

Stress originating from occupation adversely impacts physical and mental health of employees (Batista & Reio Jr., 2019).Work stress is spread across the globe, and often has adverse effect on health, general well-being, and performance based on diverse organisational and behavioural studies performed in past few decades.(Babatunde, 2013).

Literature Review
Workplace Stress

As per Pestonjee (1992) stress can originate from the following three aspects of one's life:.

- Organization and Job: This aspect of one's life talks about the work setting and the constituents which comprises of the nature of work, social relationships at workplace, work culture, organization culture, and remuneration offered at workplace.

- Social Sector: This represents social environment, and its constituents such as religion, caste, language, attitudes, political inclination of the individuals and people around him.

- Intrapsychic Sector: This aspect includes the kind of stress which can originate in the mind of an individual due to their nature or personality, values and beliefs, desires and hopes.

In both developed and developing nations, job stress is a significant health risk for workers, having impact at workplace and beyond "(Rehman et al., 2012). All those who work across organization - employees, labour, contractors, temporary workers, etc. may be impacted by stress, resulting into depression, anxiety, burnout, cardiovascular disease, and insomnia (Lee et al., 2013; Morris et al., 2013; Nakao, 2010). Such stress has further increased due to technology adoption at workplace (Gächter et al., 2011).

Job stress has significantly impacted workplace productivity – from 1996 to 2008, 1 million employees were away from the workplace each day as a result of stress and stress associated ailment – leading United Nations to label job stress as the 20th century disease. Stress has been declared as worldwide epidemic by World Health Organization (Kanji & Chopra, 2009), and thus it has become one of the most serious professional health peril (Adebayo & Ogunsina, 2011; Charu, 2013), resulting in 80% of accidents at workplace (Adaramola (2012). Overall, job stress negatively impacts worker's well-being and puts a considerable financial burden on organizational performance (Bell et al., 2012; Skakon et al., 2010). For this reason, employee health and well-being have gained significance, to drive down the compensation claims and medical costs associated with stress and stress-related illness (Nixon et al., 2011). High stress on the job has become a key issue that organizations are trying to address (Gbadamosi & Ross, 2012).

According to research conducted at The Federal Government's National Institute for Occupational Safety and Health (NIOSH) up to 40% of U.S. workers feel that their job causes stress (Feizi et al., 2012), opinion of 25% of the researched population was that their work was the prime reason for stress, opinion of 75% of the researched population was that they have increased stress at work as compared to their earlier generation (Bhui et al., 2012). According to both the gender, stress was the primary reason for people to lead an unhinged life and reaching a point of stability was their major apprehension (Matheson & Rosen 2012).

Job stress can also emanate from the role that an employee plays in an organization (Pareek, 1983). The term role was defined as a set of functions, which an employee executes in an organization based organizational and personal expectations of their role. Two role systems have been identified as part of the study which can lead to role stress.

- A conflict in the role space states that there could be struggles between the employee's role in the organization and the other roles played by them as member of a family or social structure.

- A conflict in the role set states that there could be inconsistency between the roles played by an employee in the organization and their central nature. Role set conflicts can also result from the incompatibilities within the different expectations that the roles played by other employees in the organization with the role of the individual.

With role stress impacting employees, it is imperative that a conducive environment, one which improves mental health of employees, is created at work place. Pestonjee & Pandey (2013) give introduction to the new world of work with respect to stress by highlighting issues such as:

- Necessary social structure and support system to reduce the probability of break downs in organization
- Mental health of employees at large as a result of changing social environment, technology environment, and organizational environment

Psychological Well-Being

Huppert (2009) described psychological well-being (PWB) as living with a good feeling and functioning efficiently to cope with the negative life experiences. Employee well being is a broad construct comprising of physical, psychological, and mental, health. According to Ryan & Deci (2001), some people evaluate well-being based on the nature of experiences they have in their everyday life also known as subjective well-being (SWB). While others evaluate well-being based on the existence of having significance in life and understanding its nucleus. This viewpoint of well-being which suggests how people take account of their lives is termed as psychological well-being (Waterman, 1993). The school of thought which follows subjective well-being, articulates well-being in terms of gratification in life and contentment (Diener & Suh 1997), while the school of thought which follows psychological well-being, articulates on expressions of advancement in life and existential questions of life (Ryan & Deci, 2001; Ryff, 1989, 1995).

PWB is about self-esteem, environmental mastery, autonomy, and having positive relationships resulting in purposefulness in life and getting a feeling of continued growth and development (Ryff, 1995). PWB can be defined as a mental state with a lack of a psychological condition. It can comprise of a person's aptitude to appreciate life, and ensure an equilibrium in daily happenings and to attain psychological resilience. People regularly experience moods and emotions, which have a positive effect or an adverse effect. Thus, people have a level of well-being even if they do not often perceptively think about it, and the psychological system offers a continual valuation of what is happening to the person.

Psychological well-being is tied to an individual's mindfulness that he or she has, or will have, a meaningful and self-fulfilling life (Keyes et al., 2002). PWB states in what way individuals appraise their life.

Studies show that psychological well-being can boost resilience, endurance, and optimism (Salsman et al., 2014). Psychological well-being is necessary to manage day to day life chores effectively. People find inner peace and inner gratification, which often results in reduction of stress while facing their daily life challenges.

Resilience

It refers to the psychological capacity to bounce back from misfortune, ambiguity, conflict, disaster, or any change, and increased responsibility (Luthans, 2002). According to Gu & Day (2007), resilience enables us to understand ways in which people stay motivated in times of change. Thus, resilience enables one to move on from failure and stay strong after failure.

Sirois et al., (2015) suggested that aspects such as resilience, self-compassion and mindfulness may play a part in a person's strength to sustain a constructive sense of well-being even through stressful periods. Resilience is positively associated with numerous behavioral and psychological outcomes such as positive attitude, lower suffering, and hopefulness in thinking (Kumpfer, 1999; Utsey et al., 2008). Stress resilience has been defined as the ability to rebound from stress(Smith et al., 2008), and high levels of stress resilience improves well-being at workplace"(Avey et al., 2010).

The well-being of a person can be significantly affected by their resilience (Aspinwall, 2004; Cohn et al., 2009; Tugade & Fredrickson, 2004).Based on the research by Wagnild & Young (1993), an individual's resilience can overpower the negative consequences of stress. Dyrbye et al., (2010) state that individuals with resilience experience lesser stress and depression.

While existing research backs the influence of resilience on stress, it is important to understand the relationship between resilience and role stress, further it is essential to understand whether the relationship between resilience and role stress is influenced through the mediating variable Psychological Well-being at work (PWBW). PWBW would clarify the nature of relationship between resile and role stress.

PWBW as a mediating variable between resilience and role stress may further help organisations to reduce the role stress experienced by employees.

Theoretical Framework

From this literature review, a theoretical framework is proposed which will form basis for empirical examination of the various links. The study will extend and contribute to the existing body of knowledge by prosing the following hypothesis

H1: People's resilience at work has an association with their psychological well-being at work

H2: People's role stress has an association with their resilience at work

H3: People's role stress has an association with their psychological well-being at work

H4: Psychological well-being at work mediates the negative effect of resilience on organizational role stress

Figure 1: Proposed model

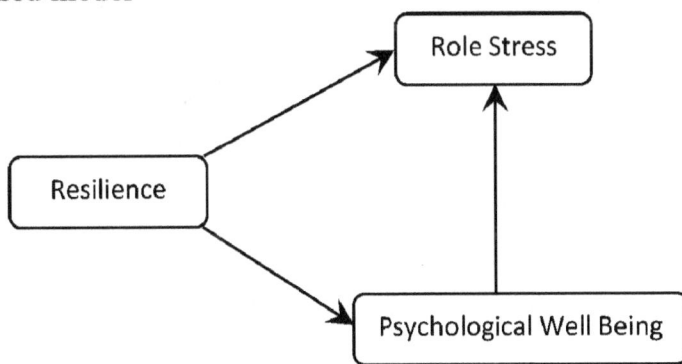

The current study aims to quantify how enhanced resilience could lead to affirmative outcomes for the individual in terms of improved psychological well-being and reduced stress.

Sample

A quantitative study on a sample of 201 employees from multiple organizations was conducted. The sample includesresponses from both the genders with 150 males and 51 females. The respondents were between the age group of 21 to 60 years with 40 percent respondents between the age group 21 to 30 and 35 percent respondents between the age group 31 to 40.

Measures

Rizzo et al., (1970) developed a scale which could measure role ambiguity and role conflict in complex organizations, however, the scale developed by Pareek (1983) called Organizational Role Stress (ORS) explores 10 dimensions of role stress which also includes role ambiguity and role conflict.

For the purpose of this study to measure role stress, Organizational Role Stress (ORS) scale (Pareek, 1983) was used. Based on the nature of the conflict (role set and role space), Organizational Role Stress was further divided into 10 types by Pareek (1983).

- A struggle between the role in the professional set up and the role in a non-professional set up i.e., with friends and family is termed as Inter-role Distance (IRD).

- When an employee feels 'stuck' in the role at the organization, they are said to have stress termed as Role Stagnation (RS).

- When a conflict arises from unwanted expectations and demands from other roles in the organization, the employee experience stress called Role Expectation Conflict (REC).

- When an employee feels the functions which their role should be performing are given to other roles, they experience stress due to Role Erosion (RE).

- When an employee feels burdened by the work assigned to their role, they experience stress due to Role Overload (RO).

- When the associations between an employee's role and the other roles in the organization are sparse/absent, they experience stress due to Role Isolation (RI).

- Personal inadequacy (PI) showcases inadequacy of skills, preparation, knowledge, of a respondent to be effective.

- When an employee is faced by conflict resulting out of their values and their role in the organization, they experience stress called Self-role distance (SRD).

- When an employee faces with lack of clarity in what other roles in the organization expect from them, they experience stress called Role Ambiguity (RA).

- When an employee has insufficient resources to perform the given task at hand, they experience stress called Resource Inadequacy (RIn).

ORS is a 50-item scale measured on five-point Likert scale with anchors ranging from 'strongly disagree' to 'strongly agree'. Of the 50 items in the scale, each of the 10 categories are measured with five items each. For the purpose of this study, the Cronbach's Alpha is 0.92.

While studying psychological well-being of employees in organizational set up, it is important to use contextualized measures because organizations have their specific concerns and practises for the employees working in it. (Dagenais-Desmarais & Savoie, 2012) introduced five dimensions of psychological well-being at work (PWBW) that designates an employee's positive experiences at work.

- The perception of an employee experiencing positive associations while networking with other employees in an organization is termed as Interpersonal fit at work (IFW).

- The perception of achieving a noteworthy and stimulating job that allows an employee to have a fulfilling exprience is termed as Thriving at work (TW).

- The awareness an employee has, of possesing the essential aptitude to do their tasks efficiently is termed as Feeling of competency (FC).

- An employee's perception that they are being appreciated in the organization is termed as Perceieved recognition (PR).

- Desire for involvement at work (DIW) is a desire of an employee to get involved in the functioning of an organization and contribute towards it's success.

It is a 25 item scale measured on seven-point Likert scale with anchors ranging from 'strongly disagree' to 'strongly agree'. Of the 25 items in the scale, each of the five categories are measured with five items each. For the purpose of this study, the Cronbach's Alpha is 0.948.

The Resilience at Work scale (Stephens et al., 2013) has been designed to assess the ability to bounce back at work. It was measured using five items (e.g., "I bounce back when I confront setbacks at work.") Items are scored on five-point rating scale (1 = strongly disagree, 5 = strongly agree). This scale has good internal consistency with Cronbach's alpha = 0.83.

Result and Analysis

Study is based on correlational research design. To examine the hypotheses, descriptive and inferential statistical methods including mean, standard deviation, correlation coefficient analysis, regression analysis, structural equation modeling through AMOS, and mediation effect with the help of bootstrapping technique.

Table 1: Descriptive Statistics

Variables	Mean	Std. Deviation	RSC	PWBW
ORS	57.428	28.157	-.259**	-.475**
RSC	5.673	1.295		.715**
PWBW	19.848	4.119		

**Significant at 0.01 level (2-tailed)

Where ORS = Organizational Role Stress, **PWBW** = Psychological Well Being at work, RSC = Resilience

Table 2: Correlations among constructs

	RSC	IRD	RS	REC	RE	RO	RI	PI	SRD	RA	RIN	IFW	TW	FC	PRW	DIW
Mean	5.673	6.910	6.537	5.065	6.726	5.866	5.861	4.925	6.174	4.214	5.149	20.229	18.891	20.592	18.761	20.766
Std. Dev.	1.295	4.026	3.869	3.548	3.571	3.788	3.613	3.656	3.688	3.662	3.442	4.299	5.177	4.173	4.794	4.105
RSC	1	-.143*	-.243**	-.297**	-0.051	-.226**	-.197**	-0.136	-.141*	-.302**	-.246**	.719**	.567**	.729**	.549**	.735**
IRD	-.143*	1	.487**	.594**	.296**	.694**	.491**	.364**	.461**	.480**	.577**	-.202**	-.244**	-.209**	-.210**	-.150*
RS	-.243**	.487**	1	.569**	.587**	.493**	.666**	.388**	.644**	.594**	.514**	-.421**	-.563**	-.353**	-.496**	-.262**
REC	-.297**	.594**	.569**	1	.389**	.651**	.596**	.493**	.615**	.716**	.715**	-.414**	-.429**	-.436**	-.431**	-.368**
RE	-0.051	.296**	.587**	.389**	1	.220**	.552**	.312**	.633**	.471**	.416**	-.236**	-.338**	-.145*	-.315**	-0.040
RO	-.226**	.694**	.493**	.651**	.220**	1	.462**	.407**	.426**	.524**	.613**	-.268**	-.294**	-.291**	-.262**	-.262**
RI	-.197**	.491**	.666**	.596**	.552**	.462**	1	.400**	.690**	.636**	.672**	-.362**	-.461**	-.286**	-.423**	-.161*
PI	-0.136	.364**	.388**	.493**	.312**	.407**	.400**	1	.564**	.595**	.532**	-.211**	-.225**	-.350**	-.266**	-.177*
SRD	-.141*	.461**	.644**	.615**	.633**	.426**	.690**	.564**	1	.676**	.652**	-.357**	-.469**	-.299**	-.442**	-.184**
RA	-.302**	.480**	.594**	.716**	.471**	.524**	.636**	.595**	.676**	1	.707**	-.443**	-.483**	-.499**	-.522**	-.354**
RIN	-.246**	.577**	.514**	.715**	.416**	.613**	.672**	.532**	.652**	.707**	1	-.337**	-.390**	-.386**	-.420**	-.262**
IFW	.719**	-.202**	-.421**	-.414**	-.236**	-.268**	-.362**	-.211**	-.357**	-.443**	-.337**	1	.800**	.788**	.812**	.815**
TW	.567**	-.244**	-.563**	-.429**	-.338**	-.294**	-.461**	-.225**	-.469**	-.483**	-.390**	.800**	1	.772**	.841**	.718**
FC	.729**	-.209**	-.353**	-.436**	-.145*	-.291**	-.286**	-.350**	-.299**	-.499**	-.386**	.788**	.772**	1	.778**	.848**
PRW	.549**	-.210**	-.496**	-.431**	-.315**	-.262**	-.423**	-.266**	-.442**	-.522**	-.420**	.812**	.841**	.778**	1	.754**
DIW	.735**	-.150*	-.262**	-.368**	-0.040	-.262**	-.161*	-.177*	-.184**	-.354**	-.262**	.815**	.718**	.848**	.754**	1

*. Correlation is significant at the 0.05 level (2-tailed).

**. Correlation is significant at the 0.01 level (2-tailed).

AMOS (Analysis of Moment Structures) was used to test the proposed relationship and to conduct data analysis among the variables. The structural equation model postulates the theorized relationship among constructs. Maximum Likelihood (ML) estimation method was used to approximate the path coefficients between the constructs.

Figure 2: Path Diagram

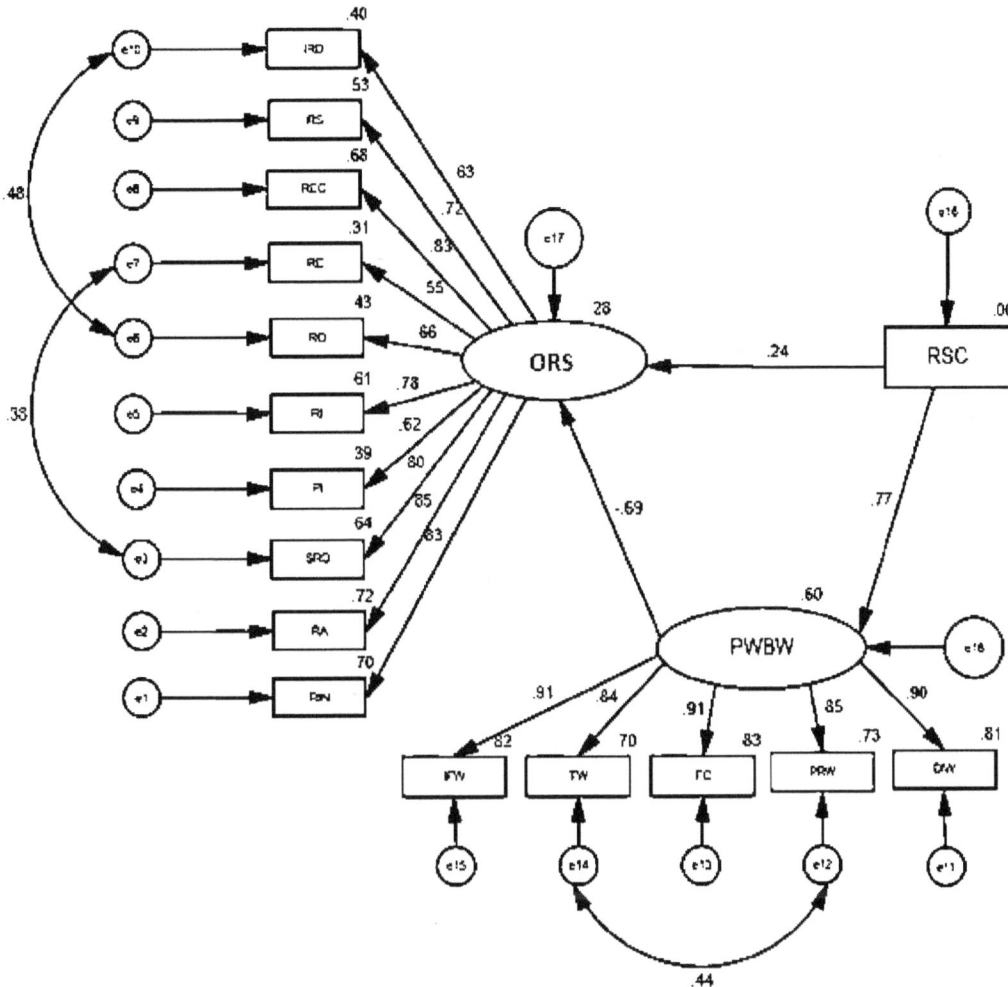

Table 3: Hypothesis testing using path coefficient

Model			Path coefficient	Remarks
H1: RSC	→	PWBW	0.774***	hypothesis supported
H2: RSC	→	ORS	0.24*	hypothesis not supported
H3: PWBW	→	ORS	-0.691***	hypothesis supported

***Significant at 0.001 level (2-tailed), *Significant at 0.05 level (2-tailed)
Where PWBW = Psychological Well Being at work, ORS = Organizational Role Stress, RSC = Resilience

Except for one path (resilience →organizational role stress), two paths were significant at 0.001 level. Data from table 1,2, and 3 show that the model provides good understanding of the aspects that impact the role stress

Table 4:
Standardized Regression Weights

			Estimate
PWBW	<---	RSC	0.774***
ORS	<---	RSC	0.24*
ORS	<---	PWBW	-0.691***
DIW	<---	PWBW	0.902***
FC	<---	PWBW	0.913***
TW	<---	PWBW	0.838***
IFW	<---	PWBW	0.905***
PRW	<---	PWBW	0.852***
RIN	<---	ORS	0.834***
RA	<---	ORS	0.848***
SRD	<---	ORS	0.8***
PI	<---	ORS	0.623***
RI	<---	ORS	0.781***
RO	<---	ORS	0.658***
RE	<---	ORS	0.553***
REC	<---	ORS	0.826***
IRD	<---	ORS	0.631***
RS	<---	Stress	0.725***

Table 5:
Squared Multiple Correlation(R^2)

	Estimate
RSC	0
PWBW	0.599
ORS	0.279
RI	0.61
RE	0.306
PI	0.388
IFW	0.819
TW	0.702
FC	0.834
PRW	0.725
DIW	0.813
IRD	0.398
RS	0.526
REC	0.683
RO	0.433
SRD	0.64
RA	0.719
RIN	0.696

***Significant at 0.001 level (2-tailed),

*Significant at 0.05 level (2-tailed)

An examination of standardized regression coefficient between the indicator and their constructs was studied to assess the convergent validity of the measurement models of the constructs. The loadings estimate varied between 0.55 and 0.85 for organizational role stress, and 0.84 and 0.91 for psychological well-being at work.

The model was verified for the likelihood of the association among the constructs. The value of χ^2 was enhanced by adding covariance among the error terms of IRD & RO and RE & SRD along with a covariance between error terms of TW & PRW. The values of fit indices were acceptable for the proposed model with GFI (goodness of fit index) = 0.790 and CFI (confirmatory fit index) = 0.895. The ratio of chi-square statistic to the degree of freedom (3.845) was less than 5.

It is estimated that resilience, as the predictor of psychological well-being, explains 60 percent of its variance. Similarly, it is estimated that psychological well-being and resilience, as the predictor of role stress explain 28 percent of its variance.

Table 6: Regression Analysis with ORS as Dependant Variable

Predictors of ORS	Zero order correlation	Standardized beta	Significance F change
Thriving at work	-0.509	-0.329	0.005
Feeling of Competency at work	-0.424	-0.288	0.023
Perceived Recognition at work	-0.494	-0.316	0.009
Desire for Involvement at work	-0.290	0.428	0.000

Total R square = 0.307, therefore, variance explained = 30.7%

The model summary indicates that there are four determinants of ORS i.e. TW, FC, PRW, and DIW. This can be expressed in the following equation where only standardized beta coefficients have been used: y = a + bx1 + bx2 + bx3 + bx4

y (dependent variable) = alpha + beta of predictor 1 + beta of predictor 2 … + beta of predictor 4.

Based on the above equation, various contributors of ORS can be placed in the following equations:

ORS = alpha + Thriving at work (-0.329) + Feeling of Competency at work (-0.288) + Perceived Recognition at work (-0.316) + Desire for involvement at work (0.428)

The table 6 reveals that desire for involvement at work is the most important predictor of ORS which explains 42.8 percent of the variance. The other predictors of ORS are thriving at work which explains 32.9 percent of the variance followed by perceived recognition at work which explains 31.6 percent variance. Feeling of competency at work explains 28.8 percent variance.

Bootstrapping method was used to understand the mediating effect of psychological well-being as bootstrapping is a preferred method to study mediation (Preacher & Hayes, 2008) given the sample size of the research is 201.

It is shown in the table 3 that the path coefficient value (for path RSC→ORS) becomes insignificant in the free model, which previously was significant ($\beta = 0.259$, $p < 0.001$) for constrain model.

Table 7: Mediation test of Psychological Wellbeing

Causal Path: PWBW as a Mediator	Path coefficient
RSC → ORS when PWBW → ORS is constrained	-0.294***
RSC → ORS when PWBW → ORS is opened	0.24

*** Significant at p< 0.001

With the help of bootstrapping technique using AMOS, the standardized indirect (mediated) effect of PWBW on RSC Stress is -.535. The bias corrected 99% confidence interval (-.771, -.333) excludes zero and therefore also supports the conclusion that the indirect effect of resilience on organizational role stress through the mediators thriving at work, feeling of competency, perceived recognition at work and desire of psychological well-being at work are statistically significant at the 0.01 level (AMOS reports the corresponding p = .004 for the bias-corrected bootstrap method). Thus, due to the indirect (mediated) effect of PWBW on RSC Stress, when RSC goes up by 1 standard deviation, Stress goes down by 0.535 standard deviations.

The discoveries from the quantitative examination helped in preparing a modified model for the study. This model redirects the association between resilience and organizational role stress and depicts psychological well-being at work as mediator. A graphic depiction of the concluding structural model, which comprises the standardized path coefficients, is demonstrated below.

Figure 3: Derived model

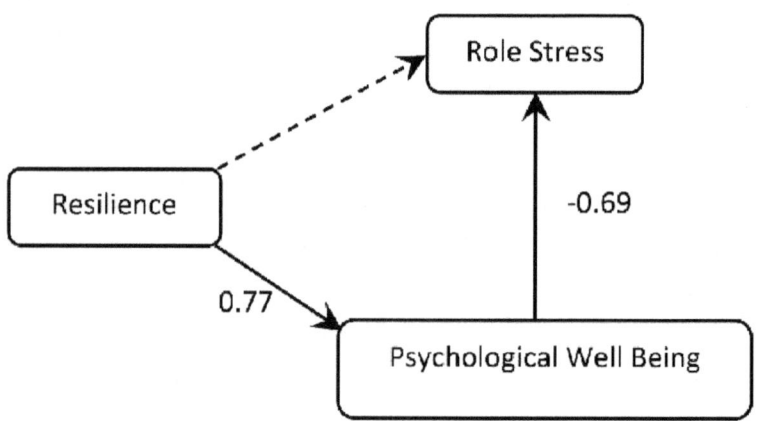

Discussions

From the path diagram and table 3, it is clear that organizational role stress has a negative relationship with an individual's psychological well-being at work. Also, resilience at work has a positive association with psychological well-being at work. These findings indicate that when an individual finds meaning and purpose in life as a result of the work, they tend to experience lower stress at workplace. Individuals who evaluate their lives positively, who are mindful that they have or will have a meaningful and a self-fulfilling work life tend to be less stressed.

Those employees who perceive that they possess necessary aptitude to do their jobs efficiently, find their job stimulating and are appreciated within the organization, and experience positive association with other employees in the organization, will be able to find a meaningful and self-fulfilling work life, consequently, reducing their stress.

Organizations can play a major role in helping their employees find meaning and purpose in life and help them bounce back from work related failure which will reduce the effect of stress on the employees.

Conclusion

The concluding research model with the satisfactory model fit was established after studying the path coefficients and mediating effect of psychological well-being at work.

The acceptance of the initial hypothesis of the study specifies that resilience has a significant positive bearing on the psychological well-being at work of an employee. This finding was persistent with other studies like that of Aspinwall (2004), Cohn et al., (2009), Tugade & Fredrickson (2004). The significant result suggests that as the resilience of an employee increases, the psychological well-being at work also increases leading to more positive experiences at work. The rejection of the second hypothesis of the study indicates that the resilience of an employee does not help in reducing the role stress of the employees.

Third hypothesis supports the relationship between psychological well-being at work and organizational role stress. This suggests that when employees have positive experiences at work and find meaning and purpose in life through their work in the organization, it results in reduced role stress.

Similar study can be undertaken for the employees working in an organization to understand their psychological well-being at work and their resilience which can in turn help predict their role stress. Organizations can make a conscious effort in providing positive experiences at work, appreciate their employees more frequently, align the work done by the employees so that they find meaning and purpose in life. Such efforts will not only help in reducing the stress of the employees but also help in optimal functioning of the employees while achieving their highest potential (Ryan & Deci, 2001; Ryff, 1989, 1995).

In addition to psychological well-being and resilience other factors such as the spiritual climate of the organization can also help predict the role stress of an individual.

References

Adaramola, S. S. (2012). Job stress and productivity increase. Work, 41(1), 2955–2958. https://doi.org/10.3233/WOR-2012-0547-2955

Adebayo, S. O., & Ogunsina, S. O. (2011). Influence of Supervisory Behaviour and Job Stress on Job Satisfaction and Turnover Intention of Police Personnel in Ekiti State Journal of Management and Strategy, 2(3), 13–20. https://doi.org/10.5430/jms.v2n3p13

Aspinwall, L. G. (2004). Dealing with Adversity: Self-regulation, Coping, Adaptation, and Health. In A. Tesser & N. Schwarz (Eds.), The Blackwell handbook of social psychology. Blackwell Publishing

Avey, J. B., Luthans, F., Smith, R. M., & Palmer, N. F. (2010). Impact of positive psychological capital on employee well-being over time. Journal of Occupational Health Psychology, 15(1), 17–28. https://doi.org/https://doi.org/10.1037/a0016998

Babatunde, A. (2013). Occupational Stress: A Review on Conceptualisations, Causes and Cure. Economic Insights-Trends & Challenges, 65(3), 73–81.

Batista, L., & Reio Jr., T. G. (2019). Occupational Stress and Instigator Workplace Incivility as Moderated by Personality: A Test of an Occupational Stress and Workplace Incivility Model. Journal of Organizational Psychology, 19(2). https://doi.org/10.33423/jop.v19i2.2042

Bell, A. S., Rajendran, D., & Theiler, S. (2012). Job stress, well being, work-life balance and work-life conflict among Australian academics. E-Journal of Applied Psychology, 8(1), 25–37. https://doi.org/10.7790/ejap.v8i1.320

Bhui, K. S., Dinos, S., Stansfeld, S. A., & White, P. D. (2012). A Synthesis of the Evidence for Managing Stress at Work: A Review of the Reviews Reporting on Anxiety, Depression, and Absenteeism. Journal of Environmental and Public Health, 1–21. https://doi.org/10.1155/2012/515874

Charu, M. (2013). Effect of Occupational Stress on QWL: Amongst the Associates of IT Industry. Advances in Management, 6(5).

Cohn, M. A., Fredrickson, B. L., Brown, S. L., Mikels, J. A., & Conway, A. M. (2009). Happiness Unpacked: Positive Emotions Increase Life Satisfaction by Building Resilience. Emotion, 9(3), 361–368. https://doi.org/10.1037/a0015952

Dagenais-Desmarais, V., & Savoie, A. (2012). What is Psychological Well-Being, Really? A Grassroots Approach from the Organizational Sciences. Journal of Happiness Studies, 13(4), 659–684. https://doi.org/10.1007/s10902-011-9285-3

Diener, E., & Suh, E. (1997). Measuring quality of life: economic, social, and subjective indicators. Social Indicators Research, 40, 189–216. https://doi.org/10.1023/A:1006859511756

Dyrbye, L. N., Power, D. V, Massie, F. S., Eacker, A., Harper, W., Thomas, M. R., Szydlo, D. W., Sloan, J. A., & Shanafelt, T. D. (2010). Factors associated with resilience to and recovery from burnout: a prospective, multi-institutional study of US medical students. Medical Education, 44(10), 1016–1026. https://doi.org/10.1111/j.1365-2923.2010.03754.x

Feizi, M., Soheili, S., Hasanzadeh, M., & Pakdel, A. (2012). Surveying the relationship between job stressors and withdrawal behaviors (in health and social security office of Ardebil city). Australian Journal of Basic and Applied Sciences, 6(9), 407–411.

Gächter, M., Savage, D. A., & Torgler, B. (2011). The relationship between stress, strain and social capital. Policing, 34(3), 515–540. https://doi.org/10.1108/13639511111157546

Gbadamosi, G., & Ross, C. (2012). Perceived Stress and Performance Appraisal Discomfort: The Moderating Effects of Core Self-Evaluations and Gender. Public Personnel Management, 41(4), 637–659. https://doi.org/10.1177/009102601204100404

Gu, Q., & Day, C. (2007). Teachers resilience: A necessary condition for effectiveness. Teaching and Teacher Education, 23(8), 1302–1316. https://doi.org/10.1016/j.tate.2006.06.006

Huppert, F. A. (2009). Psychological Well-being: Evidence Regarding its Causes and Consequences. Applied Psychology: Health and Well-Being, 1(2), 137–164. https://doi.org/10.1111/j.1758 0854.2009.01008.x

Kanji, G. K., & Chopra, P. K. (2009). Psycho-social system for work well-being: On measuring work stress by causal pathway. Total Quality Management & Business Excellence, 20(5), 563–580. https://doi.org/10.1080/14783360902875741

Keyes, C. L. M., Shmotkin, D., & Ryff, C. D. (2002). Optimizing well-being: The empirical encounter of two traditions. Journal of Personality and Social Psychology, 82(6), 1007–1022. https://doi.org/10.1037/0022-3514.82.6.1007

Kumpfer, K. L. (1999). Factors and processes contributing to resilience: The resilience framework. In M. . Glantz & J. L. Johnson (Eds.), Longitudinal research in the social and behavioral sciences. Resilience and development: Positive life adaptations (pp. 179–224). Kluwer Academic Publishers.

Lee, J.-S., Joo, E.-J., & Choi, K.-S. (2013). Perceived Stress and Self-esteem Mediate the Effects of Work related Stress on Depression. Stress and Health, 29(1), 75–81. https://doi.org/10.1002/smi.2428

Luthans, F. (2002). The need for and meaning of positive organizational behavior. Journal of Organizational Behavior, 23(6), 695–706. https://doi.org/10.1002/job.165

Matheson, J. L., & Rosen, K. H. (2012). Marriage and Family Therapy Faculty Members' Balance of Work and Personal Life. Journal of Marital and Family Therapy, 38(2), 394–416. https://doi.org/10.1111/j.1752-0606.2009.00137.x

Morris, M. L., Messal, C. B., & Meriac, J. P. (2013). Core Self-Evaluation and Goal Orientation: Understanding Work Stress. Human Resource Development Quarterly, 24(1), 35–62. https://doi.org/10.1002/hrdq.21151

Nakao, M. (2010). Work-related stress and psychosomatic medicine. BioPsychoSocial Medicine, 4, 1–8. https://doi.org/10.1186/1751-0759-4-4

Nixon, A. E., Mazzola, J. J., Bauer, J., Krueger, J. R., & Spector, P. E. (2011). Can work make you sick? A meta-analysis of the relationships between job stressors and physical symptoms. Work and Stress, 25(1), 1–22. https://doi.org/10.1080/02678373.2011.569175

Pareek, U. (1983). Group and Organization Studies. Sage Publications, Inc.

Pestonjee, D. M. (1992). Stress and Coping: The Indian Experience. Sage Publications, Inc.

Pestonjee, D. M., & Pandey, S. (2013). Stress and Work Perspectives on Understanding and Managing Stress. Sage Publications, Inc.

Preacher, K. J., & Hayes, A. F. (2008). Contemporary Approaches to Assessing Mediation in Communication Research. In The SAGE Sourcebook of Advanced Data Analysis Methods for Communication Research (pp. 13–54). Sage Publications, Inc. https://doi.org/10.4135/9781452272054.n2

Rehman, M. ur, Rabbia, I., Tahir, N., Ijaz, Z., Noor, U., & Ume, S. (2012). The Impact of Job Stress on Employee Job Satisfaction: A Study on Private Colleges of Pakistan. Journal of Business Studies Quarterly, 3(3), 50–56.

Rizzo, J. R., House, R. J., & Lirtzman, S. I. (1970). Role Conflict and Ambiguity in Complex Organizations. Administrative Science Quarterly, 15(2), 150. https://doi.org/10.2307/2391486

Ryan, R. M., & Deci, E. L. (2001). On happiness and human potentials: A review of research on hedonic and eudaimonic well-being. Annual Review of Psychology, 52(February), 141–166. https://doi.org/10.1146/annurev.psych.52.1.141

Ryff, C. D. (1989). Happiness is everything, or is it? Explorations on the meaning of psychological well-being. Journal of Personality and Social Psychology, 57(6), 1069–1081. https://doi.org/10.1037/0022-3514.57.6.1069

Ryff, C. D. (1995). Psychological Well-Being in Adult Life. Current Directions in Psychological Science, 4(4), 99–104. https://doi.org/10.1111/1467-8721.ep10772395

Salsman, J. M., Lai, J.-S., Hendrie, H. C., Butt, Z., Zill, N., Pilkonis, P. A., Peterson, C., Stoney, C. M., Brouwers, P., & Cella, D. (2014). Assessing psychological well-being: self-report instruments for the NIH Toolbox. Quality of Life Research, 23(1), 205–215. https://doi.org/10.1007/s11136-013-0452-3

Sirois, F. M., Kitner, R., & Hirsch, J. K. (2015). Self-compassion, affect, and health-promoting behaviors. Health Psychology, 34(6), 661–669. https://doi.org/10.1037/hea0000158

Skakon, J., Nielsen, K., Borg, V., & Guzman, J. (2010). Are leaders' well-being, behaviours and style associated with the affective well-being of their employees? A systematic review of three decades of research. Work and Stress, 24(2), 107–139. https://doi.org/10.1080/02678373.2010.495262

Smith, B. W., Dalen, J., Wiggins, K., Tooley, E., Christopher, P., & Bernard, J. (2008). The brief resilience scale: Assessing the ability to bounce back. International Journal of Behavioral Medicine, 15(3), 194–200. https://doi.org/10.1080/10705500802222972

Stephens, J. P., Heaphy, E. D., Carmeli, A., Spreitzer, G. M., & Dutton, J. E. (2013). Relationship Quality and Virtuousness: Emotional Carrying Capacity as a Source of Individual and Team Resilience. Journal of Applied Behavioral Science, 49(1), 13–41. https://doi.org/10.1177/0021886312471193

Tugade, M. M., & Fredrickson, B. L. (2004). Resilient Individuals Use Positive Emotions to Bounce Back From Negative Emotional Experiences. Journal of Personality and Social Psychology, 86(2), 320–333. https://doi.org/10.1037/0022-3514.86.2.320

Utsey, S. O., Giesbrecht, N., Hook, J., & Stanard, P. M. (2008). Cultural, Socio-familial, and Psychological Resources That Inhibit Psychological Distress in African Americans Exposed to Stressful Life Events and Race-Related Stress. Journal of Counseling Psychology, 55(1), 49–62. https://doi.org/10.1037/0022-0167.55.1.49

Wagnild, G. M., & Young, H. M. (1993). Development and psychometric evaluation of the Resilience Scale. Journal of Nursing Measurement, 1(2), 165–178.

Radhika Thanki is pursuing PhD from School of Petroleum Management, Pandit Deendayal Energy University, Gandhinagar. She can be reached at thanki.radhika@gmail.com.

D M Pestonjee, PhD, is currently associated with School of Petroleum Management, Pandit Deendayal Energy University, Gandhinagar, as GSPL Chair Professor since July 2009. He served the Indian Institute of Management, Ahmedabad for over two decades (1979-2001) as professor of Organizational Behaviour. He can be reached at pestonjee@hotmail.com

Dynamic Interaction Between Nifty 50 and Nifty Sectoral Indices: An Empirical Study on Indian Stock Indices

K Ramya
Assistant Professor (SS), Department of Business Administration
Avinashilingam Institute for Home Science and Higher Education for Women, Coimbatore, India.

Bhuvaneshwari D
Assistant Professor, Department of Humanities
PSG College of Technology, Coimbatore, India.

Received 13 July 2020
Revised 19 October 2020
Accepted 11 March 2021

Abstract

This study aims to determine the cointegrating and causal relationship between Nifty 50 and Nifty sectoral indices. Historical index data of the select indices were collected from the National Stock Exchange (NSE) database for the period Jan 2014 - Dec 2018. Appropriate Econometric tools - Augmented Dickey-Fuller (ADF) test, Phillips and Perron (PP) test, regression model, Granger causality test, and Johansen cointegration test were used to analyze the data. The findings of the study imply that the movements of Nifty sectoral index prices could determine the flow of stock index prices, i.e., Nifty 50 and vice versa during the period of the study which could also help the policymakers and financial planners in providing financial awareness to investors and clients in decision making.

Keywords: Nifty 50, Nifty Sectoral Indices, Indian Stock Indices, Granger Causality, Johansen Cointegration

Introduction

The stock market prices are considered as an essential indicator of a country's economic and social status and are seen as a leading indicator of real economic activity. The countries with better economic growth have better stock market performance (Duca 2007).Economic growth plays a vital role in the stock market development in both developing and developed economies. The development of the stock market does not solely depend upon the macroeconomic indicators because the sectoral contribution towards the market growth also causes significant development in the stock market. The stock market suffers from various typical weaknesses of an emerging market such as high market volatility, lack of transparency, and infrastructure bottlenecks, which led most of the researchers to study the cointegration and causality of macroeconomic variables on the broad stock indices. This study identified that the researches focusing on the aggregate effect of sectoral stock indices on the Nifty 50 index prices is of rarity.

The study focuses on the sectoral indices of Nifty namely, Nifty Auto, Nifty Bank, Nifty Financial Services, Nifty FMCG, Nifty IT, Nifty Media, Nifty Metal, Nifty Pharma, Nifty Pharma, Nifty Pharma, Nifty Private Bank, Nifty PSU Bank and Nifty Realty indices because the sectoral indices are designed to reflect the behaviour and performance of the respective sectors. Each index comprises of stocks that are listed in NSE. The list of stocks indexed in Nifty sectoral indices as of Nov 2019 is given in Annexure 1. These stocks for the index were selected based on detailed eligibility criteria structured by NSE. Therefore, it becomes vital to study the relationship between Nifty sectoral and Nifty 50 index prices. The aim of this study is to determine the cointegrating and causal relationship between the study variables and to find the impact of Nifty sectoral index prices on Nifty 50. This study is expected to offer valuable insights to investors to make informed decisions about sectoral stock indices and to help the policymakers and financial planners in providing financial awareness to investors and clients.

Literature Review

Several studies have been carried out in developed stock markets such as the United States (US), United Kindom (UK), Germany, and Japan; examples of pioneer studies are Fama (1981, 1990), Geske and Roll (1983), and Chen, Roll, and Ross (1986). These studies were found to vary in terms of the methodology adopted and the hypotheses. The literature that demonstrated the relationships between the stock indices are: Chiang and Doong (2001) analyzed the time-series behavior of stock returns for seven Asian stock markets by using Threshold Autoregressive GARCH. After testing the relationship between stock returns and unexpected volatility, the evidence showed that four out of seven Asian stock markets have significant results. Lee, Chen and Rui (2001) examined the time series features of stock returns and volatility, as well as the relation between return and volatility in four of China's stock exchanges. Variance ratio tests rejected the hypothesis that stock returns follow a random walk, and the study found evidence of long memory of returns. Application of GARCH and EGARCH models to the study provided strong evidence of time varying volatility and showed volatility is highly persistent and predictable.

Berben and Jansen (2005) investigated shifts in correlation patterns among international equity returns at the market level as well as the industry level using the weekly data from Germany, Japan, the UK, and the US in the period 1980 - 2000. A novel bivariate GARCH model for equity returns with a smoothly time-varying correlation and then derive a Lagrange Multiplier statistic from testing the constant correlation hypothesis was developed. The study found that correlations among the German, UK and US stock markets have doubled, whereas Japanese correlations have remained the same. Giot (2005) found that there was a negative and statistically significant relationship between the returns of the S&P 100 and the NASDAQ 100 stock indexes and their corresponding implied volatility indexes, VIX and VXN. For the S&P 100, the relationship is asymmetric, as negative stock index returns were more associated than positive returns with greater changes in VIX. VIX changes when negative stock index returns were observed were greater in low-volatility periods. The study also found that positive, forward-looking returns were to be expected for long positions triggered by extremely high levels of the implied volatility indexes.

Li, Yang, Hsiao and Chang (2005)determined the issue of co-movement between stock markets in major developed countries and those in Asian emerging markets using the concept of cointegration. The study found that there exists a co-movement between some of the developed and emerging markets, but some emerging markets do differ from the developed markets with which they share a long-run equilibrium relationship. Phylaktis and Ravazzolo (2005) examined the stock market linkages of a group of Pacific-Basin countries with the US and Japan by estimating the multivariate cointegration model in both the autoregressive (AR) and moving average (MA) forms over the period 1980 - 1998. The results for the 1980s indicated that the relaxation of foreign ownership restrictions was not sufficient to attract foreign investors' attention, and those other factors must have affected the portfolio diversification decision. The results of the 1990s suggested that the relaxation of the restrictions might have strengthened international market interrelations.

A study by Hasan and Javed (2009) explored the long-term relationship between Pakistan equity prices and monetary variables and provided evidence of a long-run relationship and unidirectional Granger causality between the equity market and monetary variables. Dimitriou and Simos(2011) empirically investigated the relationship between expected stock returns and volatility in the twelve EMU countries as well as five major out of EMU international stock markets for the period 1992 - 2007 using GARCH models. The study found a weak relationship between expected returns and volatility for most of the markets and also identified unravels significant evidence of a negative relationship in almost all markets.

Data

The analytical method of research was adopted for this study as the cause and effect of Nifty 50 movements are explained with Nifty sectoral indices using the historical data of the indices, i.e., secondary data. The data were collected from the National Stock Exchange (NSE) database for five years from Jan 2014 to Dec 2018. The selections of indices were based on the availability of data and the requirement of a good number of observations, which are essential for studies on time series. The indices considered for the study are Nifty 50 (broad index) and Nifty sectoral indices namely Nifty Auto, Nifty Bank, Nifty Financial Services, Nifty FMCG, Nifty IT, Nifty Media, Nifty Metal, Nifty Pharma, Nifty Pharma, Nifty Pharma, Nifty Private Bank, Nifty PSU Bank and Nifty Realty. The unit of measurement of all the study variables is index prices. The acronym of the study variables used in the analyses and tables in this research are Nifty 50 →N50; Nifty Auto →NAuto; Nifty Bank→NBank; Nifty Financial Services → NFinServ; Nifty FMCG →NFMCG; Nifty IT →NIT; Nifty Media→NMedia; Nifty Metal →NMetal; Nifty Pharma →NPharma; Nifty Private Bank →NPrivate; Nifty PSU Bank →NPSU and Nifty Realty → NRealty. The list of stocks indexed in Nifty 50 and Nifty sectoral indices as of Nov 2019 are given in Annexure 1. The methodology of the study is provided in the following section.

Methodology

This research study is based on the standard method of causality and cointegration tests. Specifically, the empirical framework of this study involves various steps. First, by using the Augmented Dickey-Fuller (ADF) and Phillips and Perron (PP) tests, each series is tested for unit roots. Secondly, the regression model was framed to forecast future responses. Thirdly, to assess their causal nexus empirically, Granger causality test was used, and finally, to test for cointegration among the stock indices, the maximum likelihood approach was performed using the Johansen cointegration approach. The analyses for this study were conducted using Eviews 7 software.

Objective And Hypotheses

The objective of this study is as follows:

❖ To determine the short-run and long-run relationship between Nifty 50 and Nifty sectoral indices.

The following hypotheses are set to test the above objectives empirically:

❖ H01: There is no significant short-run relationship existing between Nifty 50 and Nifty sectoral indices.

❖ H02: There is no significant long-run relationship existing between Nifty 50 and Nifty sectoral indices.

Analysis And Interpretation

This section discusses the preliminary analysis, which includes descriptive statistics and unit root tests. Subsequently, the results from the detailed system analysis are presented, which include the regression model, the Granger causality test, and the Johansen cointegration test.

Descriptive Statistics: The descriptive statistics of the select stock indices for the study period are presented in Table 1. The result shows that there is a large difference between the minimum and maximum values of the indices. It is also identified that there are fluctuations in the movement of prices and have grown rapidly during the study period.

Table 1 - Descriptive Statistics

Particulars	N50	NAuto	NBank	NFinServ	NFMCG	NIT	NMedia	NMetal	NPharma	NPrivate	NPSU	NRealty
Mean	8817.88	9025.48	19879.74	8179.74	22549.46	11411.30	2586.13	2808.29	10293.63	10928.11	3185.52	223.21
Median	8532.85	8841.85	18825.15	7695.40	21063.80	11097.90	2519.35	2805.15	10359.90	10266.74	3185.45	210.65
Maximum	11738.50	12009.70	28320.00	11838.10	32911.55	16234.90	3642.70	4195.75	13831.15	16088.90	4419.25	372.25
Minimum	6000.90	4912.40	10102.10	4313.50	16336.10	8675.10	1655.15	1495.60	7411.60	5147.47	1968.00	128.25
Std Deviation	1321.94	1675.85	4502.20	1892.22	3954.17	1521.22	479.37	660.82	1479.30	2747.04	501.17	52.24
Skewness	0.18	-0.34	0.07	0.19	0.64	1.14	0.06	-0.02	0.05	0.05	-0.14	0.56
Kurtosis	2.26	2.51	2.09	2.05	2.29	3.88	2.01	2.04	2.17	2.08	2.69	2.43
Jarque-Bera	34.70***	36.35***	43.08***	53.75***	108.84***	306.08***	51.21***	47.12***	36.20***	43.74***	8.83***	81.21***
Observations	1233	1233	1233	1233	1233	1233	1233	1233	1233	1233	1233	1233

*** Significant at the 1% level

The skewness is positive (right-skewed) for select indices, namely Nifty 50, Nifty Bank, Nifty Financial Services, Nifty FMCG, Nifty IT, Nifty Media, Nifty Pharma, Nifty Private Bank and Nifty Realty which means that the mean is greater than the mode. The skewness is negative (left-skewed) for indices, namely Nifty Auto, Nifty Metal and Nifty PSU Bank, which means that the mean is less than the mode. This further suggested that the movements of the select indices are related to one another and are found to be systematic. The kurtosis coefficient values for Nifty IT was found to be positive and greater than 3, which indicates that the distribution to be leptokurtic. The kurtosis coefficient values for all the select indices except Nifty IT were positive and found to be less than 3, which indicated that the distribution to be platykurtic with fewer and less extreme outliers. Subsequently, the Jarque-Bera test statistics suggest that all the select indices namely Nifty 50, Nifty Auto, Nifty Bank, Nifty Financial Services, Nifty FMCG, Nifty IT, Nifty Media, Nifty Metal, Nifty Pharma, Nifty Pharma, Nifty Pharma, Nifty Private Bank, Nifty PSU Bank and Nifty Realty were statistically significant at 1% level and were not normally distributed.

Testing the Data for Stationarity: The results for the ADF and PP unit root tests for checking the stationarity of the data are presented in Table 2.

Table 2 - Results of ADF and PP Unit Root Tests (with constant and trend)

Study Variables	ADF Unit Root Test		PP Unit Root Test	
	Level	First Difference	Level	First Difference
N50	-1.29	-32.56***	-1.30	-32.48***
NAuto	-2.23	-32.84***	-2.23	-32.80***
NBank	-1.13	-33.51***	-1.14	-33.48***
NFinServ	-0.84	-33.90***	-0.83	-33.88***
NFMCG	-0.53	-34.05***	-0.47	-34.08***
NIT	-1.10	-34.23***	-1.10	-34.23***
NMedia	-1.78	-33.54***	-1.76	-33.54***
NMetal	-1.18	-34.36***	-1.18	-34.35***
NPharma	-2.04	-32.13***	-2.01	-32.13***
NPrivate	-1.10	-33.86***	-1.10	-33.84***
NPSU	-2.53	-34.03***	-2.55	-34.02***
NRealty	-1.66	-32.42***	-1.52	-32.40***

*** Significant at the 1% level

From Table 2 results, it is identified that all the select indices were found to be stationary at first difference series. Hence, all the time series data are statistically significant and integrated at order I(1). Therefore, it is understood that the sample data taken for this study are stationary, i.e., predictable.

Time Series Regression: It is a statistical method used in this study to forecast the future response of the Indian stock index prices based on past data of select economic indicators. The result of time series regression is presented in Table 3.

Table 3 - Estimation of the Regression Model

Independent Variables	Coefficient	Std. Error	t Statistics	R Square	Adjusted R Square	F Statistics
Constant	903.11	39.78	22.70***			
NAuto	0.11	0.01	17.92***			
NBank	0.06	0.02	2.63***			
NFinServ	0.27	0.03	10.55***			
NFMCG	0.06	0.00	22.28***			
NIT	0.10	0.00	34.48***	0.998	0.998	58518.68**
NMedia	-0.14	0.01	-11.31**			
NMetal	0.24	0.01	32.12***			
NPharma	0.06	0.00	17.99***			
NPrivate	-0.02	0.03	-0.68			
NPSU	0.02	0.02	0.96			
NRealty	1.39	0.09	15.16***			

*** Significant at the 1% level

The regression output consists of four important information: (a) the R2 value which is based on the sample and represents the proportion of variance in Nifty 50 index prices that can be explained by the Nifty sectoral indices and it indicates the fitness of the regression model. For a model to be fit, the R2 value is said to be 0.60 or above. In this study, the estimated parameters of the equation obtained were found to be statistically significant, with a R2 value of 0.998, as shown in Table 3.

The predictor variables explained about 99.8 percent of the change in Nifty 50 index prices. An adjusted R2 value corrects the positive bias to provide a value that could be expected in the population. The adjusted R2 value of the model is 0.998, which is found to have zero variation from the R2 value. The F value of the model is 58518.68, which indicated that the model is statistically significant at the 0.01 level, and the coefficients for the constant and independent variables, i.e., Nifty sectoral indices are the information used to construct a model and forecast the dependent variable, i.e., Nifty 50 index prices. The regression equation derived from the results:

$$N50_t = 903.11 + 0.11\ (NAuto) + 0.06\ (NBank) + 0.27\ (NFinServ) + 0.06\ (NFMCG) \\ + 0.10\ (NIT) - 0.14\ (NMedia) + 0.24\ (NMetal) + 0.06\ (NPharma) \\ - 0.02\ (NPrivate) + 0.02\ (NPSU) + 1.39\ (NRealty) + e$$

Testing for Granger Causality: Granger causality test is used in this study to determine the causality between the study variables, i.e., to check whether Nifty 50 is useful in forecasting the Nifty sectoral indices and vice versa and also helps in determining the short-run equilibrium relationship. The results of the Granger causality test for Nifty 50 and Nifty sectoral indices are given in Table 4.

Table 4 - Results of Granger Causality Test (Nifty 50 and Nifty SectoralIndex Prices)

Null Hypotheses	F Value	Results
NAuto does not Granger Cause N50	0.15	Accept
N50 does not Granger Cause NAuto	1.65	Accept
NBank does not Granger Cause N50	4.00**	Reject
N50 does not Granger Cause NBank	0.85	Accept
NFinServ does not Granger Cause N50	3.90**	Reject
N50 does not Granger Cause NFinServ	1.68	Accept
NFMCG does not Granger Cause N50	1.95	Accept
N50 does not Granger Cause NFMCG	0.67	Accept
NIT does not Granger Cause N50	2.24	Accept
N50 does not Granger Cause NIT	3.66**	Reject
NMedia does not Granger Cause N50	0.23	Accept
N50 does not Granger Cause NMedia	2.53	Accept
NMetal does not Granger Cause N50	2.88	Accept
N50 does not Granger Cause NMetal	3.78**	Reject
NPharma does not Granger Cause N50	7.79***	Reject
N50 does not Granger Cause NPharma	2.21	Accept
NPrivate does not Granger Cause N50	2.99**	Reject
N50 does not Granger Cause NPrivate	0.88	Accept
NPSU does not Granger Cause N50	0.82	Accept
N50 does not Granger Cause NPSU	0.91	Accept
NRealty does not Granger Cause N50	0.45	Accept
N50 does not Granger Cause NRealty	1.96	Accept

Note: Appropriate lag length was determined by the Akaike information criterion.
***Significant at 1% level, **Significant at 5% level

The direction of causality is found to be unidirectional and significant in the following cases: Nifty Bank→Nifty 50; Nifty Financial Services→Nifty 50; Nifty 50 →Nifty IT; Nifty 50→Nifty Metal; Nifty Pharma →Nifty 50 and Nifty Private Bank→Nifty 50. Therefore, Hypothesis H01, there is no significant short-run relationship existing between Nifty 50 and Nifty sectoral indices is rejected and inferred that causality and the short-run relationship is found between Nifty 50 and Nifty sectoral index prices. It is also found that the sectoral indices namely, Nifty Bank, Nifty Financial Services, Nifty Pharma and Nifty Private Bank indices have had an impact on Nifty 50 index prices, whereas, Nifty IT and Nifty Metal index prices had a significant impact due to changes in the Nifty 50 index prices during the short-run period.

Testing for the Existence of a Long-run Equilibrium Relationship: Johansen's cointegration test is applied to find the stationary linear combination and long-run cointegrating equilibrium among the study variables. The results of the trace test and maximum eigenvalue test are presented in Table 5.

Table 5 - Results of Johansen's Cointegration Test (Nifty 50 and Nifty Sectoral Index Prices)

H_0	N50		5% Critical Value	
	Trace Value	Maximum Eigen Value	Trace Value	Maximum Eigen Value
r = 0	353.33**	65.00	334.98	76.58
r ≤ 1	288.33**	58.08	285.14	70.54
r ≤ 2	230.25	51.91	239.24	64.50
r ≤ 3	178.34	44.54	197.37	58.43
r ≤ 4	133.80	36.12	159.53	52.36
r ≤ 5	97.68	26.74	125.62	46.23
r ≤ 6	70.94	22.00	95.75	40.08
r ≤ 7	48.93	15.17	69.82	33.88
r ≤ 8	33.76	12.63	47.86	27.58
r ≤ 9	21.13	10.04	29.80	21.13
r ≤ 10	11.09	7.49	15.49	14.26
r ≤ 11	3.60	3.60	3.84	3.84

Note: P Values were estimated by MacKinnon-Haug-Michelis (1999)
**Significant at the 5% level

The result of the cointegration tests indicates the existence of a long-run equilibrium relationship among the study variables. Two cointegrating vector equations were found between Nifty 50 and Nifty sectoral index prices. Therefore, Hypothesis H_{02} as there is no significant long-run relationship existing between Nifty 50 and Nifty sectoral indices is rejected and inferred that there exists a long-run equilibrium relationship between the study variables, which means that the select variables can be forecasted by past (historical) values of other variables considered for the study.

Conclusion

The present study is an attempt to analyze and estimate the impact of Nifty sectoral indices on Nifty 50 index prices. The variables used for the study were stationary at their first difference with the order of integration I(1). It was found that Granger causality, i.e., the short-run relationship existed between the study variables. Therefore, it can be concluded that this study partially supports the 'Complementarity Hypothesis' propounded by McKinnon's (1973). Further, it could also be inferred that the long-run cointegrating relationship existed between Nifty 50 and Nifty sectoral index prices. The managerial implications of the present study are that the movements of Nifty sectoral index prices could determine the flow of stock index prices, i.e., Nifty 50 and vice versa, during the period of the study. The study also establishes that all the policies regarding Nifty sectoral indices have immediate changes in the behavior of Nifty 50. Further, the study provides implications to policymakers regarding lead indicators of the stock market to formulate suitable policies and strategies in the future. It could identify the lead sectoral indices that have a significant impact on Nifty 50 index prices, which could also help the policymakers and financial planners in providing financial awareness to investors and clients in decision making.

References

Berben, R. P., & Jansen, W. J. (2005). Comovement in international equity markets: A sectoral view. *Journal of International Money and Finance*, 24(5), 832-857. https://doi.org/10.2139/ssrn.457961

Chen, N. F., Roll, R., & Ross, S. A. (1986). Economic forces and the stock market. *Journal of Business*, 59(3), 383-403. https://doi.org/10.1086/296344

Chiang, T. C., & Doong, S. C. (2001). Empirical analysis of stock returns and volatility: Evidence from seven Asian stock markets based on TAR-GARCH model. *Review of Quantitative Finance and Accounting, 17*(3), 301-318. https://doi.org/10.1023/a:1012296727217

Dimitriou, D., & Simos, T. (2011). The relationship between stock returns and volatility in the seventeen largest international stock markets: A semi-parametric approach. *Modern Economy, 1*(2), 1-8. https://doi.org/10.4236/me.2011.21001

Duca, G. (2007). The relationship between the stock market and the economy: experience from international financial markets. *Bank of Valletta Review, 36*(3), 1-12.

Fama, E. F. (1981). Stock returns, real activity, inflation, and money. *The American Economic Review, 71*(4), 545-565. https://doi.org/10.2307/2328716

Fama, E. F. (1990). Stock returns, expected returns, and real activity. *The Journal of Finance, 45*(4), 1089-1108. https://doi.org/10.1111/j.1540-6261.1990.tb02428.x

Geske, R., & Roll, R. (1983). The fiscal and monetary linkage between stock returns and inflation. *The Journal of Finance, 38*(1), 1-33. https://doi.org/10.2307/2327635

Giot, P. (2005). Relationships between implied volatility indexes and stock index returns. *The Journal of Portfolio Management, 31*(3), 92-100. https://doi.org/10.3905/jpm.2005.500363

Hasan, A., & Javed, M.T. (2009). An empirical investigation of the causal relationship among monetary variables and equity market returns. *The Lahore Journal of Economics, 14*(1), 115-137. https://doi.org/10.35536/lje.2009.v14.i1.a5

Lee, C. F., Chen, G. M., & Rui, O. M. (2001). Stock returns and volatility on China's stock markets. *Journal of Financial Research, 24*(4), 523-543. https://doi.org/10.1111/j.1475-6803.2001.tb00829.x

Li, Q., Yang, J., Hsiao, C., & Chang, Y. J. (2005). The relationship between stock returns and volatility in international stock markets. *Journal of Empirical Finance, 12*(5), 650-665. https://doi.org/10.1016/j.jempfin.2005.03.001

Phylaktis, K., & Ravazzolo, F. (2005). Stock market linkages in emerging markets: Implications for international portfolio diversification. *Journal of International Financial Markets, Institutions and Money, 15*(2), 91-106. https://doi.org/10.2139/ssrn.562922

Historical Index Data (n. d.), National Stock Exchange (NSE). Retrieved from https://www.nseindia.com/products/content/equities/indices/historical_index_data.htm, Retrieved on Nov 2019.

Annexure - 1
Stocks Listed in Nifty 50 and Nifty Sectoral Indices

S.No.	Indices	Number of Companies	List of Companies
1	N50	50	Adani Ports and Special Economic Zone, Asian Paints, Axis Bank, Bajaj Auto, Bajaj Finance, Bajaj Finserv, Bharat Petroleum Corporation, Bharti Airtel, Bharti Infratel, Britannia Industries, Cipla, Coal India, Dr. Reddy's Laboratories, Eicher Motors, GAIL (India), Grasim Industries, HCL Technologies, HDFC Bank, Hero MotoCorp, Hindalco Industries, Hindustan Unilever, Housing Development Finance Corporation, ICICI Bank, ITC, Indian Oil Corporation, IndusInd Bank, Infosys, JSW Steel, Kotak Mahindra Bank, Larsen & Toubro, Mahindra & Mahindra, Maruti Suzuki India, NTPC, Nestle India, Oil & Natural Gas Corporation, Power Grid Corporation of India, Reliance Industries, State Bank of India, Sun Pharmaceutical Industries, Tata Consultancy Services, Tata Motors, Tata Steel, Tech Mahindra, Titan Company, UPL, UltraTech Cement, Vedanta, Wipro, Yes Bank and Zee Entertainment Enterprises
2	NAuto	15	Amara Raja Batteries, Apollo Tyres, Ashok Leyland, Bajaj Auto, Bharat Forge, Bosch, Eicher Motors, Exide Industries, Hero MotoCorp, MRF, Mahindra & Mahindra, Maruti Suzuki India, Motherson Sumi Systems, TVS Motor Company and Tata Motors
3	NBank	12	Axis Bank, Bank of Baroda, Federal Bank, HDFC Bank, ICICI Bank, IDFC First Bank, IndusInd Bank, Kotak Mahindra Bank, Punjab National Bank, RBL Bank, State Bank of India and Yes Bank
4	NFinServ	20	Axis Bank, Bajaj Finance, Bajaj Finserv, Bajaj Holdings & Investment, Cholamandalam Investment and Finance Company, Edelweiss Financial Services, HDFC Bank, HDFC Life Insurance Company, Housing Development Finance Corporation, ICICI Bank, ICICI Lombard General Insurance Company, ICICI Prudential Life Insurance Company, Indiabulls Housing Finance, Kotak Mahindra Bank, Mahindra & Mahindra Financial Services, Power Finance Corporation, REC, SBI Life Insurance Company, Shriram Transport Finance Co. and State Bank of India
5	NFMCG	15	Britannia Industries, Colgate Palmolive (India), Dabur India, Emami, Godrej Consumer Products, Godrej Industries, Hindustan Unilever, ITC, Jubilant Foodworks, Marico, Nestle India, Procter & Gamble Hygiene & Health Care, Tata Global Beverages, United Breweries and United Spirits
6	NIT	10	HCL Technologies, Hexaware Technologies, Infosys, Justdial, MindTree, NIIT Technologies, Tata Consultancy Services, Tata Elxsi, Tech Mahindra and Wipro
7	NMedia	15	Balaji Telefilms, D.B.Corp, Dish TV India, Hathway Cable & Datacom, Inox Leisure, Jagran Prakashan, Music Broadcast, Network18 Media & Investments, PVR, Saregama India Ltd, Sun TV Network, TV Today Network, TV18 Broadcast, Zee Entertainment Enterprises and Zee Media Corporation
8	NMetal	15	APL Apollo Tubes, Coal India, Hindalco Industries, Hindustan Copper, Hindustan Zinc, JSW Steel, Jindal Steel & Power, MOIL, NMDC, National Aluminium Co., Ratnamani Metals & Tubes, Steel Authority of India, Tata Steel, Vedanta and Welspun Corp
9	NPharma	10	Aurobindo Pharma, Biocon, Cadila Healthcare, Cipla, Divi's Laboratories, Dr. Reddy's Laboratories, Glenmark Pharmaceuticals, Lupin, Piramal Enterprises and Sun Pharmaceutical Industries
10	NPrivate	10	Axis Bank, City Union Bank, Federal Bank, HDFC Bank, ICICI Bank, IDFC First Bank, IndusInd Bank, Kotak Mahindra Bank, RBL Bank and Yes Bank
11	NPSU	12	Allahabad Bank, Bank of Baroda, Bank of India, Canara Bank, Central Bank of India, Indian Bank, Jammu & Kashmir Bank, Oriental Bank of Commerce, Punjab National Bank, State Bank of India, Syndicate Bank and Union Bank of India
12	NRealty	10	Brigade Enterprises, DLF, Godrej Properties, Indiabulls Real Estate, Mahindra Lifespace Developers, Oberoi Realty, Phoenix Mills, Prestige Estates Projects, Sobha and Sunteck Realty

Source: National Stock Exchange (NSE) as on Nov 2019

Dr K Ramya working as an Assistant Professor (SS) in the Department of Business Administration, Avinashilingam Institute for Home Science and Higher Education for Women, Coimbatore. She can be reached at krishrum9@gmail.com

Dr Bhuvaneshwari D working as an Assistant Professor in the Department of Humanities, PSG College of Technology, Coimbatore. She can be reached at bhuvaneshwaridheyvendhren@gmail.com

Cross-Cultural Dissimilarities in the Perception of Brand Personality of Select Smart phones: Evidence from West Bengal, India and Bangladesh

Shaunak Roy
Assistant Professor, Faculty of Management, Department of Commerce and Management Studies, St. Xavier's College, Kolkata

Shivaji Banerjee
Former Head and Assistant Professor, Faculty of Management, Department of Commerce, St. Xavier's College, Kolkata

Received 10 October 2020
Revised 20 December 2020
Accepted 9 March 2021

Abstract

The study has been conducted in the adjoining regions of West Bengal and Bangladesh (erstwhile East Bengal) among various respondent groups. Both the regions have been archetypally known to share multiple cultural commonalities. Notwithstanding, there exists divergences in the culture, which have been tested using Hofstede's Cultural Dimensions Framework. Further, the study investigates whether there exist any divergences in how the personalities of the two smart phone brands, namely, Samsung and Xiaomi, are perceived in the two regions. An aggregate sample of 295 and 287 respondents have been selected conveniently from West Bengal, India and Bangladesh, respectively.

The current study primarily aims to probe into the cultural dissimilarities between the two contiguous regions of West Bengal (in India) and Bangladesh. Subsequently, the study investigates the probable impact of such cross-cultural dissimilarities on consumers' perception concerning the personality of select smart phone brands, specifically Samsung and Xiaomi. The study provides good empirical insight into the fact that despite the uniform positioning of the two smart phone brands in the two West Bengal and Bangladesh regions, their personality traits are perceived differently by consumers dwelling in these cultures. The analysis yields that respondents from West Bengal and Bangladesh demonstrated notable congruencies in perceiving Xiaomi as a 'responsible' and "aggressive' brand. However, Samsung is perceived as an 'aggressive' brand in Bangladesh and 'stable' in West Bengal. The perceptual deviations of the smart phone brands' personalities exist due to the cultural divergences between the two regions.

The current study is unique in that it offers a new-fangled perspective to looking at cross-cultural research by comparing politico-administrative units instead of countries at large. Yet, it is bound by imperfections, such as limited sample size, making it difficult to make more detailed comments on individuals' perceptions towards the brand personality dimensions of smart phones. Although adequate care has been taken to eliminate the "made-in image" of the Chinese smart phones, respondents were generally biased towards the product quality, brand acquaintance and their overall perceptions towards the personality of the said brands.

Brand personality plays an integral role in easing communications with customers. They can, resultantly, relate conveniently to the identity and the personality traits possessed by such brands. Marketing professionals can essentially aim to foster a brand-customer personality congruence, which would ideally enable them to position their product offerings accordingly and design tailored advertising and marketing communication messages. A well-defined brand personality initiates greater customer purchase willingness coupled with amplified emotional attachment, trust and loyalty, thereby enhancing the significance of branding to managers. They can help develop frameworks to analyze behavioral intentions concerning consumer perception of brand personality.

Keywords: Cross-cultural; Brand Personality; West Bengal; Bangladesh; Smart Phone Brands

Introduction

The idea of leveraging brands to create a distinguishing impact in the minds of target consumers is not new, especially since it helps gain formidable competitive advantage "(D. A. Aaker, 1991; Holt, 2010; Kapferer, 1996; Mason & Batch, 2009). In fact, consumers often look upon brands as valuable implements that assist them in expressing their personality employing their purchase decisions and actual purchase acts (Cătălin & Andreea, 2014; Kim et al., 2001). Hence, it is of new relevance for branding professionals to develop robust marketing communications programs, such that the target consumers can engage with their preferred brands, both meaningfully and efficaciously.

In this context, brand personality has often been used by marketers as a novel and valuable implement to distinguish their products from competing brands (Åberg, 2015; Kim et al., 2001), and consequently establish brand equity (Ahmad & Thyagaraj, 2015a; Gorbaniuk et al., 2015). Brand personality has been defined as "a set of human characteristics that are associated with a specific brand." (J. L. Aaker, 1997). Resultantly, consumers who strongly relate to the personality of their preferred brands can make improved and more informed brand choices and demonstrate better brand usage trajectories (Ambroise et al., 2004; Su & Tong, 2015; Tessa, 2018). Furthermore, brand personality as a construct helps marketing specialists to develop more effectual branding strategies by better comprehending the inherent emotive and symbolic connotations that are ascribed to brands by consumers. Research has observed that brand personality has a positive influence on active "customer engagement" (Yasin et al., 2020), as well as a significant influence on "brand love" (Anggraenia & Rachmanita, 2015; Roy et al., 2016). In recent times, the application of brand personality has been found extensively in the case of travel and tourism (Ekinci & Hosany, 2006; Usakli & Baloglu, 2011), as well as niche realms such as Islamic marketing (Ahmed & Jan, 2015; Zainudin et al., 2019). These explorations suggest that there remain several other product and service categories where the applications of brand personality are yet to be explored.

However, literature data continues to be lacking in the case of consumer electronics. Although brand personality scales have been previously applied to measure the authenticity of consumer electronics such as smartphones (Chung & Park, 2017), typically applying the frameworks advanced by J.L. Aaker(1997), such studies have focussed on the application of the scale in a specific regional context (Sundar & Noseworthy, 2016) or among students in a given institutional context (Ajilore & Solo-Anaeto, 2016). Several reasons justify the rationale for the selection of smart phones. Backed by rising income levels, India's holistic demand for consumer durables has been soaring. Other factors such as "rising rural incomes", "expanding urbanisation", an "emerging middle class", and "changing lifestyles" are expected to support demand growth in the market (Rajeswari & Pirakatheeswari, 2014; Sathya & Vijayasanthi, 2016). Today, across the world, the market for smart phones has been observed to be exceedingly competitive, especially in light of the breakneck technological innovations and product differentiations that have resulted in the dynamism visible in the industry (Cecere et al., 2015; Ngoc Anh, 2016; Paul & Cornelia, 2019). The market dominance rests in the hands of a few global smart phone brands, which try to position themselves uniformly within various regional market contexts (Khandelwal, 2019). Yet, one of the significant bottlenecks faced by managers of smart phone brands happens to be the proper understanding of cultural divergences that have a prospective influence on how the personality of such brands is perceived across two or more countries or geographic regions.

Interestingly, brand managers can develop a unique brand personality and position it uniformly across consumers in different cultures through the effective use of promotional tools, packaging strategies, signs, symbols and other brand artefacts (Staplehurst & Charoenwongse, 2012; Zadeh & Rose, 2018). The present study presents a unique opportunity to fathom the unique opportunities available to smart phone brands in nurturing their businesses beyond a national boundary. Smart phone brands have genuinely become global brands today (Silver, 2019), and it is crucial to recognize the dynamics of customers dwelling in different nations and geographical regions in terms of several socio-demographic aspects, perceptions, attitudinal attributes, value and belief systems. Such a profound insight would aid in the comprehension of global smart phone brands such as Samsung, Xiaomi, Apple, among other brands.

In the current study, the neighbouring regions of West Bengal (India) and Bangladesh have been considered. The selection is primarily driven by the fact that the two cultures share relatively similar cultures, be it in terms of language, art or music. Several studies corroborate the rationale for the selection of the two regions (Rahman et al., 2019). A profound insight into the smart phone markets of the two regions helps in strengthening the understanding of the rationale for selecting the two neighbouring regions, wherein the customer adoption and diffusion of smart phones has seen a significant surge since the last decade(Press Trust of India Report, 2020; Shifat, 2020). The trajectories of smart phone ownership in both regions are also similar in many ways. Around 74 per cent of the urban population of Bangladesh were found to own smart phones, out of which nearly three-fifths of the populace happened to possess internet-enabled devices (Bayes, 2019). On the other hand, 61 per cent of the urban population in West Bengal are known to use internet-enabled smart phones (Press Trust of India, 2013). West Bengal also accounts for an excess of 5 per cent of the entire smart phone production in India, with an estimated monthly production capacity of nearly 5 lakh smart phones(Raj, 2020).

From a theoretical perspective, it may be argued that regions bearing similar cultures may demonstrate commonalities in the manner in which the brand personality of consumer electronic products such as smart phones are perceived by consumers dwelling in both cultures (Hanel et al., 2018; J. Karlin & Weil, 2019; Norenzayan et al., 2002). Previous studies have shown that in regions with heterogeneous cultures, the personality of a specific brand may not be perceived uniformly in tandem with how the company initially conceived it because such cultural divergences have some bearing on the cultural connotations ascribed to the brand in respective regions (Chegini et al., 2016; Foscht et al., 2008a; Jansson, 2013; Tunkkari, 2017). Such inconsistencies in perceptions may pose a challenge for regiocentric and geocentric market-orientated companies to develop global marketing strategies to maintain an unswerving brand image to ensure success in world markets.

One of the most effective frameworks to probe into the cultural meaning of a specific region is the framework developed by Geert Hofstede in 1980, which has been accepted globally as a uniform paradigm to probe into inherent cultural divergences. There are six dimensions proposed in the framework, which mutually depict the cultural impact entrenched in a given region in terms of the value structures held by the members belonging to the said region. They are "Power Distance Index", "Uncertainty Avoidance", "Individualism vs Collectivism", "Masculinity vs Femininity", "Long-Term vs Short-Term Orientation", and "Indulgence vs Restraint". To comprehend the cultural connotations of the brand personality construct across the neighbouring regions of West Bengal and Bangladesh, it is also crucial to establish a liaison with Hofstede's cultural dimensions (Jansson, 2013; Matzler et al., 2016; Phau & Lau, 2000).

Research Objective

Accordingly, the current study attempts to probe into the following research questions:

RQ1: Are there any cultural dissimilarities between the two contiguous regions of West Bengal, India and Bangladesh?

Rq2: Is the personality of Samsung and Xiaomi smart phone brands perceived differently across the two cultures of West Bengal and Bangladesh?

RQ3: Do the cultural dimensions of each region (viz. Bangladesh and West Bengal) have any significant impact on the perception of brand personality of Samsung and Xiaomi?

Literature Review

The academic inquest in brand personality has acquired significant status in recent times, as marketing professionals seek to distinguish their brands from their rivals and develop a competitive advantage. Although global brands are positioned uniformly across diverse cultures, there are differences in how they are perceived across diverse cultures. The review of background literature has been categorized under the several extensive domains covered in the study.

Brand Personality Dimensions

Over time, there has been adequate evidence to establish that brand personality as a construct acts as a valuable implement in examining the behaviour of consumers (Bairrada et al., 2019; Chovanová et al., 2015). Brand personality is regarded as a crucial element of brand identity theory (Lindeberg et al., 2012; Phau & Lau, 2000; Rajagopal, 2012; Robertson et al., 2019; Shyle & Hysi, 2013), and it is defined as "the set of human personality traits that are both applicable to and relevant for brands" (Azoulay & Kapferer, 2003). This definition encompasses not only demographic components such as age, gender and social class, but also distinctive personality traits such as "excitement", "ruggedness", "sincerity", "competence" and "sophistication" much like human beings (J. L. Aaker, 1997). It is not merely a means to establish the physical traits linked by consumers with their preferred brands, but a unique approach to uncover the brand preferences made by them coupled with their deep-rooted emotional states in correlation with specific brands (J. L. Aaker, 1997; Ahmad & Thyagaraj, 2015a; Bozbay & Ozkan, 2016).

Brands which possess unique personality traits are known to acquire profound meaning in the minds of the consumers, and thereby acquire human-like attributes over time (MacInnis & Folkes, 2017; Puzakova et al., 2009; Puzakova & Kwak, 2017). The only distinction is that unlike human personality, which is ordinarily deep-rooted and ingrained as a core component of individual behaviour itself, the personality of a brand, au contraire, is subject to how it is perceived by individuals in the process of brand contact, that is to say, from procuring and using the said brand (Ahmad & Thyagaraj, 2015b; Maehle et al., 2011; Milas & Mlačić, 2007; Pandey, 2009; Srivastava & Sharma, 2016). The representative personality traits are essentially shaped in the consumer of a said brand, as the versatile personality facets are transmitted to the brand in question (Arsena et al., 2014; Becheur et al., 2017; Sheena & Naresh, 2012). Furthermore, the distinctive attributes of the brand's top management are also rubbed off onto the said brand in many a few cases (Keller & Richey, 2006; Robertson et al., 2019). Such transmission of traits consequents in the personification of a brand, with a sui generis character of its own.

In the recent past, there have been an array of studies that have corroborated that the perception of brand personality varies according to multiple cultures (Geuens et al., 2009; Gondim Mariutti & de Moura Engracia Giraldi, 2019; Khandai et al., 2015; Kumar, 2018; Sung et al., 2015). For instance, in a study by Muniz & Marchetti (2012), a 28-item inventory of personality traits was derived in the Brazilian context instead of the scales developed in the milieu of other countries and cultures. Similarly, Srivastava & Sharma (2016) endeavoured to validate the Aaker's scale in India's telecom services, wherein they observed that the 'sophistication' dimension was not a robust fit with the theoretical model of brand personality. In yet another study by Bishnoi & Kumar (2016), it was concluded that ten items from Aaker's novel brand personality scale did not hold in their entirety in the context of bikes in India. The study reasoned that triggers such as product deviants and socio-cultural attributes were responsible for the inconsistency with the primal scale, with even archetypal human attributes not being validated to the brand in focus. Some of the critical papers have been summarized in Table 1.

Table - 1 : Key Papers on Brand Personality

Author(s) & Year	Research Objective(s)	Methodology	Main Conclusion(s)	Criticisms of the Study
Aaker, J. L. (1997)	Development of a theoretical framework of the brand personality construct by determining the number and nature of brand personality dimensions	Survey Method; Scale Development & Validation using PCA and CFA	Creation of a reliable and valid five-factor, 42-item measurement scale for brand personality (sincerity, excitement, competence, sophistication, and ruggedness)	[1] The scale is a crude measure of brand personality as it transposes human personality traits rather than using brands themselves [2] The model is American-specific as it did not always receive empirical substantiation across different cultural settings
Fournier, S. (1998)	[1] Examines the validity of the relationship proposition in the consumer-brand context [2] Development of a framework for characterizing the types of relationships consumers form with brands [3] Establish the concept of brand relationship quality	In-depth Cross-Case Study Analysis	[1] Holistic character of consumer-brand relationship phenomena [2] Insight into how brand personality is created, developed and changed over time	[1] Failure to accurately represent how consumers interact with brands [2] While consumers may attribute anthropomorphic traits to brands, it does not imply that socio-psychological aspects of interpersonal relationships are adequate to represent consumer-brand liaisons
Geuens, M., Weijters, B. & De Wulf, K. (2009)	Development of a new brand personality measure consisting of personality items only (as a clear amelioration over Aaker's BPS)	Survey method; Scale development & validation using EFA and CFA	Creation of a reliable, valid and generalisable five-factor, 12-item measurement scale for brand personality (responsibility, activity, aggressiveness, emotionality, simplicity)	[1] An exclusive data-centric approach to retain items resulting in the deletion of key traits as they did not associate with any dimension [2] The cross-cultural validity of the new BPS remains a problem [3] Nomological validity remains to be investigated
Heine, K. (2012)	[1] Attempt to define the personality of luxury brands [2] Outlining the requirements and selection criteria for luxury brand personality traits	A consumer-oriented qualitative method including Repertory Grid Method developed by Kelly, G. (1955); Content analysis to fathom personality dimensions	[1] Establishment of five personality dimensions to define luxury brands (modernity, eccentricity, opulence, elitism, and strength) [2] Creation of a framework for the analysis of emotional luxury brand images	[1] The study is German-focussed; hence its validity across other cultures is highly debatable [2] The study is biased, as it involves the researcher's subjective interpositions

The personality traits tend to differ across multiple cultural contexts because of the divergences in how they are positioned (Olsson & Sandru, 2006). Although branding professionals endeavour to sustain uniform patterns of marketing communications and other marketing strategies across the world, it is dubious whether a singular tone of voice developed by the concerned brand would yield desired results (Staplehurst & Charoenwongse, 2012). Hence, the key is to comprehend the cultural connotation in which the brands are expected to communicate with their target customers.

Cultural Dimensions

Culture may be understood as "the collective programming of the mind distinguishing the members of one group or category of people from others" (Hofstede, 2011). Culture as a construct encompasses an array of components such as language (Sepora et al., 2012), symbols (Shen, 2017), religion (Beyers, 2017), values, norms, practices (Pereira et al., 2015), artefacts (Hopes, 2014) and standards. Such parameters have been identified to impact several facets of human behaviour and their decision-making competencies (Cronk, 2017; Ford, 1942; Wang et al., 2006). More importantly, culture has also been observed to significantly impact how individuals develop perceptual cues towards various product and service offerings (Overby et al., 2005; Shavitt & Barnes, 2020). Consumers belonging to a specific culture can better accept brands if the marketing communications and promotional programs of a given brand are in sync with their cultural perceptions of the said culture. However, one of the significant problems crippling cross-cultural research is that methodological issues and financial constraints render it highly arduous to assess the cultural impact in predicting the extent of individual purchase and consumption behaviour of the individuals in the said region (Caprar et al., 2015).

On this note, one of the pioneering studies that attempted to quantify multiple cultures across several dimensions was the framework developed by Hofstede (1980), which paved a new avenue to identify and analyze the divergences that may or may not exist among national cultures. Hofstede's seminal framework has been criticized heavily by several authors in the past (Eringa et al., 2017; Jones, 2007; McSweeney, 2002; Williamson, 2002), primarily since culture does not parallel with countries as such, and resultantly, the model culminates in oversimplifying the culture of a broad array of countries. Critics contend that it would be feasible only if individual social orders are secluded from one other. Yet, the framework stands tall today, as a widely accepted framework in academic and corporate circles, in competently measuring the dimensions of culture across multiple countries in the world (Zainuddin et al., 2018). The current study has adopted the 6-D Model of National Culture, which encompasses six dimensions highlighted by Hofstede in his updated framework on measuring national culture, namely "Power Distance Index", "Uncertainty Avoidance Index", "Individualism vs Collectivism", "Masculinity vs Femininity", "Long-Term Orientation vs Short-Term Orientation" and "Indulgence vs Restraint". It may be noted that the cultural dimensions reflect a representation of the self-directed predilections for one setup over another that helps differentiate countries. In fact, the scores obtained post measurement happen to be relative, and thus culture can essentially be utilized evocatively through such comparison. The six dimensions of the model are summarized in Table 2.

Table 2: Summary of Hofstede's Dimensions of National Culture and their Primary Characteristics

Cultural Dimension	High Score	Low Score
Power Distance Index	Individuals accede to a hierarchical order wherein everybody has a place that requires no additional validation	Individuals strive to even out the power distribution and demand validation for disparities of power dynamics
Uncertainty Avoidance Index	Individuals are known to uphold unyielding belief systems and behavioural trajectories while demonstrating bigotry towards unconventional behaviours and ideas	Individuals are known to uphold a more easy-going attitude in which practice counts more than established ideologies
Individualism vs Collectivism	Individuals prefer to have an unrestricted social framework wherein they are expected to take care of solely themselves and their direct kin	Individuals prefer to have a compact societal framework wherein they can expect their kinsfolks or members of a precise ingroup to take care of them for wholehearted dependability
Masculinity vs Femininity	Individuals generally exhibit penchants for accomplishment, heroism, decisiveness, competitiveness and material rewards for success	Individuals generally exhibit preferences for consensus-centric activities, collaboration, diffidence, caring for the weak and quality of life
Long-Term vs Short-Term Orientation	Individuals are known to adopt more matter-of-fact tactics as they promote prudence and endeavours in innovative educational access as a means to make ready for the future	Individuals prefer to maintain longstanding traditions and norms while observing societal transformation with several misgivings
Indulgence vs Restraint	Indulgence-focussed societies are tolerant of moderately uninhibited gratification of rudimentary and innate individual drives associated with appreciating life and deriving exuberance	Restraint-focussed societies are known to subdue fulfilment of innate individual needs and controls them through the provision and implementation of stringent societal norms and practices

Relationship between Cross-Cultural Dimensions and Brand Personality

A selection of values and demands may be established within a specific cultural construct, which demonstrates the importance of brand perceptions, and consequently, culture-oriented variations in brand personality are expected to surface (Jansson, 2013). Specific attributes of brand personality may have an analogous connotation across cultures, while others may possess culturally unique meanings (Vellnagel, 2020). There also exist several cultural variations in terms of the symbolic usage of brands in different product and service contexts (Matzler et al., 2016). Further, in a study by Parks & Tong (2020), it was observed that the brand personality of lifestyle brands in Southern regions of the USA was perceived as "sophisticated", "casual", and "Southern". Furthermore, consumers from the Southern states of the USA are more inclined to procure regionalized products, and consumers perceive such brands as having propitious traits. Owing to specific backgrounds, lifestyles, and customs, a consumer's country of origin positively impacts their brand assessment and choice.

It is clear that existing literature that erstwhile studies have attempted to explain whether cultural differences exist among countries and whether such differences impact the perception of brand personality (Foscht et al., 2008a). However, it must be noted that given culture and a country are not synonymous. In other words, a country may possess multiple cultures. For instance, India is a country with multiple cultures and subcultures (Dheer et al., 2015). Yet, there exist commonalities in cultures between, say, Punjab in India and Punjab in Pakistan (Chordia, 2016) or between Kerala in India and Sri Lanka (Balachandran, 2006). Where earlier studies fall short by considering entire countries and nations as distinct cultural units, the current study attempts to make a bold leap by exploring the similarities and dissimilarities in culture between the politico-administrative state of West Bengal (in eastern India) and the neighbouring country of Bangladesh. More pertinently, the study is a first attempt to throw light on the differences in perception that may or may not exist between the two cultures concerning the brand personalities of two top smart phone brands and whether the cultural dimensions influence such perceptions. The conceptual framework ensuing from the study objectives have been delineated in Figure 1.

Figure : Conceptual Model adopted for the Study
(Source: Adopted from Geuens et al., 2009 & Hofstede, G. (2011)

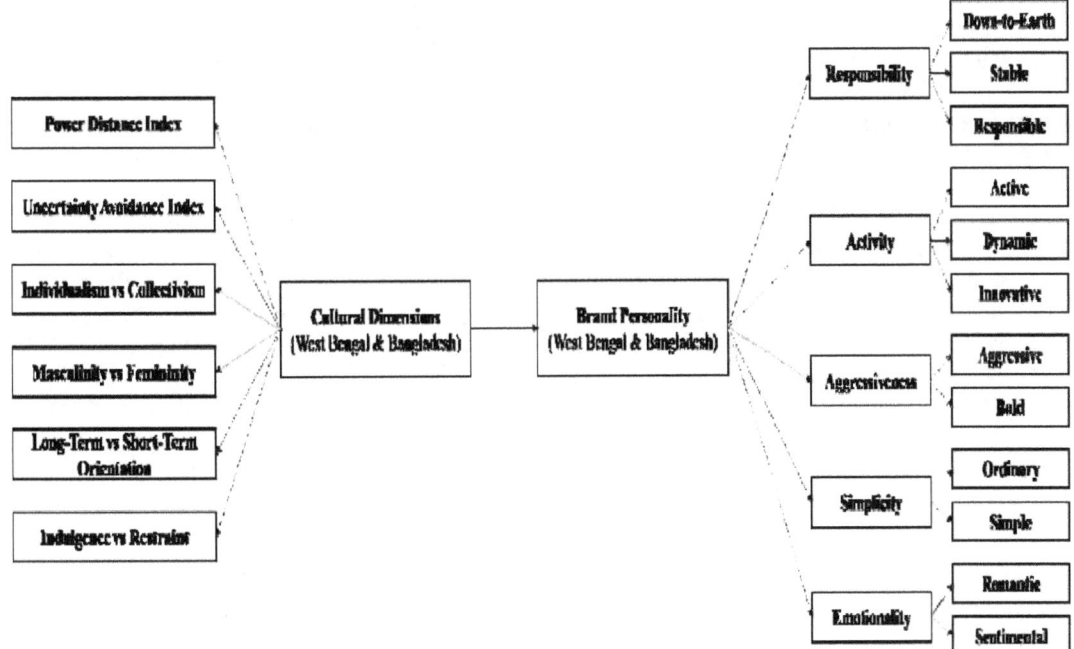

As mentioned earlier, the study's primary purpose is to examine whether the cultural dimensions in the neighbouring regions of West Bengal and Bangladesh influence the perception of brand personality for the selected smart phones, namely, Samsung and Xiaomi. The study also probes into the viable differences between the perceptions of brand personality in the two regions and cultural dimensions.

Methodology

The current study employed a five-stage framework (Figure 1), based on the insights developed by Malhotra et al. (1996), to conduct the cross-cultural analysis in the two neighbouring regions of West Bengal and Bangladesh (Figure 2).

Figure : Methodology adopted in the Current Study

[Source: Based on the Framework developed by Malhotra et al. (1996)]

STAGE I Defining the Research Problem	STAGE II Framing the Emic/Etic Approach	STAGE III Developing the Research Design	STAGE IV Sorting Data Analysis Issues	STAGE V Presentation & Interpretation of Data
Ensuring relevance in comparing perceptions of Brand Personality	Emic and etic approach used for the evaluation of consumer attitudes towards cultural dimensions as well as perceptual study on assessing brand personality conducted in West Bengal (India) and Bangladesh respectively	Employing a survey-based instrument for data collection	Ensuring sample comparability	Presentation of Data
Minimizing complexities by isolating the Self-Reference Criterion (SRC)		Establishing construct equivalence (functional, conceptual, instrument and measurement)	Preparing and standardizing data across the two cultures	Interpretation of Data

The first methodological consideration was to ensure that the construct of brand personality is comparable across the two cultures, and more importantly, the two cultures may at all be comparable. West Bengal is a state in India, while Bangladesh is a country. Although it seems implausible that the two regions cannot be compared due to the apparent incongruity in political and administrative demarcations, there exists logical feasibility in comparing the two neighbouring regions. To understand the rationale, the historical backdrop of the two regions must be investigated. Notwithstanding, the most apparent reason for selecting Bangladesh and West Bengal is the manifest Bengali ethnicity among the majority of the populace. Although national divergences warrant discrete units of politico-administrative divisions, the two regions follow a dominant democratic political system. The year 1947 witnessed India gaining independence from British colonial rule. Concurrently, the British-Indian administrative province of Bengal was segregated, based on religious divergences, into the Hindu-dominant West Bengal and the Islam-dominant East Pakistan (which eventually became Bangladesh in the wake of the Bangladesh Liberation War of 1971). Before the partition in 1947, the present-day region representing Bangladesh was referred to as East Bengal (or Purbô Bangla) —belonging to the same geographic region of British-administered India. Today, West Bengal and Bangladesh share multiple commonalities in terms of cultural variables. For instance, the two regions predominantly converse in the Bengali language, despite the apparent linguistic divergences in pronunciations, lexicons or morphology in the dialect.

To a great extent, even the food preferences in the two cultures are similar to each other. Both cultures

Table -3 West Bengal Vs. Bangladesh (Socio-Economic Variables)

Defining Element		West Bengal (India)	Bangladesh
Dominant Ethnicity		Bengali	Bengali
Political System		Parliamentary (Federal) Democratic Republic	Parliamentary (Representative) Democratic Republic
Official Language		Bengali; English	Bengali; English
Population		9.13 crores (2011 est.)	14.23 crores (2011 est.)
Urban Population		2.91 crores (2011 est.)	4.44 crores (2016 est.)
Literacy Rate		76.26% (2011 est.)	47.68% (2011 est.)
HDI Value		0.641 (2018 data)	0.614 (2018 data)
Religion	*Hinduism*	70.54% (2011 est.)	8.54% (2011 est.)
	Islam	27.01% (2011 est.)	90.39% (2011 est.)
	Other	2.45% (2011 est.)	1.07% (2011 est.)
Minimum Wages (Monthly)	Unskilled	USD 109.89	USD 67.40
	Skilled	USD 146.27	USD 90.18

The study has been conducted from an emic as well as an etic perspective. When conducted in the context of Bangladesh, the study adopts an etic approach, as the researchers did not integrate or immerse themselves in the local culture being observed, despite the apparent commonalities. The key is to ensure that the indigenous culture is not interfered with during the conduct of the study. While the study remains anonymous and the respondent data is treated with utmost confidentiality, there remains a probability that respondents from Bangladesh might provide responses differently while being surveyed. Hence, the researchers have sought the assistance of two post-graduate students from Bangladesh in administering the survey and mitigate the difficulties associated with adopting an etic approach to a great extent.

On the other hand, when the study has been conducted in West Bengal, India, an emic assessment of culture has been adopted, where the inherent cultural idiosyncrasies relevant to the people of West Bengal have been focussed upon. Since the researchers themselves are inhabitants of West Bengal, a detailed probe into the societal norms and cultural beliefs of West Bengal have been considered, which might otherwise have been ignored. However, adequate care has been taken to ensure that, when adopting an emic perspective in conducting the research, self-reference criterion (SRC) does not emanate. This would potentially trigger significant cultural misinterpretations on account of the researchers' unconscious reference to their fundamental cultural values prevalent in West Bengal whilst exploring the culture of Bangladesh (Lee, 1966). Cross-cultural taxonomies tend to be either sheer inventories (Fan, 2000; Triandis, 1989) or exceedingly conjectural intricate arrangements (Chick, 1997). Since there exists a generally acknowledged dearth of a comprehensive and global structure within which national cultures may be envisaged, the framework conceptualized by Hofstede (1980, 2011) and Hofstede & Bond (1984) stands tall as one of the most effective measures for conducting cross-cultural analysis, while taming the prevailing issues of ethnocentrism and SRC.

Further, in the context of cross-cultural studies, it is almost imperative that construct equivalence be established in terms of its functional and conceptual attributes and measurement quantities (Kankaraš & Moors, 2010; Tomas et al., 1995; Trimble, 2010). Both West Bengal and Bangladesh are known to be heavy users of smartphone brands and hence tend to develop unique perceptions towards the personality of such brands. Functional equivalence exists because of the apparent commonalities in terms of demonstrated consumer behaviour in the two cultures, despite the possibility of behavioural divergences. Next, conceptual equivalence is also established, as the dimensions of culture developed by Hofstede remains uniform across the two cultures, in addition to the construct of brand personality. The research problem in the current study has thus been defined so that it is not culture-constrained and essentially remains conceptually equivalent for respondents in the two cultures being investigated (West Bengal and Bangladesh). Instrument equivalence has also been established by ensuring that the versatile items in the brand personality scale, response groupings and the inducements in the structured questionnaire (smartphone brands considered, consumer behaviour, positioning strategies of brands) are interpreted unvaryingly in the two cultures. Linguistic equivalence has been established as English has been used as the common medium of written and verbal communication in the questionnaire comprising items categorised under Hofstede's Cultural Framework and the brand personality scale. Translations into the

Bengali language were not necessitated for any of the respondents in the context of the current study. Finally, scalar equivalence has also been established in that the scores obtained from the respondents in West Bengal and Bangladesh share identical connotations and construal. In essence, it may be feasible to represent equivalences and conduct a cross-cultural analysis to investigate consumer perceptions towards the brand personality construct of smartphones in the adjoining geographical regions of West Bengal and Bangladesh (Buil et al., 2012; Malhotra et al., 1996).

Selection of Brands

Using the Counterpoint Research Report 2019 as a foundation, the current study considers two among the top five smartphone brands that are commonly used and recognized by respondents in both West Bengal and Bangladesh, namely, Samsung and Xiaomi (Choudhary, 2019; Jain, 2019). The top-selling smartphone brand in Bangladesh is "Samsung" (market share of 22% in Q1 2019), followed by "Symphony" (market share of 16% in Q1 2019), "Transsion" and "Walton" (market share of 9% each in Q1 2019). However, brands such as Symphony, Transsion and Walton are not available in West Bengal and the Indian market. The next most selling smartphone brand in Bangladesh is "Xiaomi" (market share of 7% each in Q1 2019). In the Indian context, the top smartphone brands happen to be "Xiaomi" (market share of 26% in Q3 2019), followed by "Samsung" (market share of 20% in Q3 2019). Since these two top-selling brands are common to both regions, they have been considered in the present study. The sample comprised participants from various age groups in the two regions, namely West Bengal (n=295) and Bangladesh (n=287). A fair and adequate share of participants from various age cohorts was profiled and surveyed, primarily since users of the two smartphone brands mentioned earlier are disseminated across such age segments. The respondents were administered a structured questionnaire comprising three segments, namely, Segment A (comprising questions about the demographic profile of respondents), Segment B (comprising questions on the Hofstede's Cultural Dimensions) and Segment C (comprising questions on the perceptions of respondents towards the brand personality of Xiaomi and Samsung smartphones). The scale comprises close-ended questions on a 5-point Likert scale, ranging from "Strongly Agree" to "Strongly Disagree"

Selection of Brand Personality Scale

As specified earlier, the novel scale developed by Geuens et al. (2009) has been used to measure brand personality instead of the Aaker's scale (1997). The superiority of the former measure has been deliberated upon in former studies (Alpatova & DallOlmo, 2011). The scale comprised of 12 items, as opposed to the 44-item instrument in the seminal study. The reliability statistics of the new brand personality scale have been summarized in Table 4. The five-brand personality factors considered in the study are "responsibility" (encompassing traits such as "down-to-earth", "stable", and "responsible"), "activity" (encompassing traits such as "active", "dynamic" and "innovative"), "aggressiveness" (encompassing traits such as "aggressive" and "bold"), "simplicity" (encompassing traits such as "ordinary" and "simple"), and "emotionality" (encompassing traits such as "romantic" and "sentimental"). A 62-item structured questionnaire based on the framework developed by Hofstede (2011) has been employed to measure the cultural divergences between West Bengal and Bangladesh. It would help determine how respondents perceive the culture in which they dwell. The questionnaire comprised of six segments, which are summarized below in Table 4:

Table 4: Reliability Analysis Results for the Variables in the Hofstede's Framework (2011)

Constructs	Cronbach's Alpha		No. of Items
	India	Bangladesh	
Variables in the Hofstede's Framework			
Power Distance Index	0.946	0.929	10
Uncertainty Avoidance Index	0.937	0.948	13
Individualism vs Collectivism	0.893	0.919	8
Masculinity vs Femininity	0.921	0.898	14
Long-Term vs Short-Term Orientation	0.932	0.921	9
Indulgence vs Restraint	0.918	0.973	8
Variables in the Brand Personality Scale			
Responsibility	0.897	0.797	3
Activity	0.932	0.872	3
Aggressiveness	0.839	0.891	2
Simplicity	0.837	0.913	2
Emotionality	0.893	0.938	2

The questionnaire also comprised questions about consumer behaviour in terms of smartphone purchases in the two regions. Respondents were preliminarily asked if they were current users of the Samsung or Xiaomi brands to ensure the robustness of the data generated. Slovin's formula is given as "$n = N / (1+N \times e^2)$", where "n=sample size", "N=total population", and "e=margin of error". The present study determines its sample size with 95 per cent confidence with an error margin of 5 per cent. Accordingly, a sample size of approximately 277 participants in both West Bengal and Bangladesh is sufficient to draw meaningful generalizations in the study. The sample size in the present study is 295 respondents in the case of West Bengal and 287 in Bangladesh. The study has eliminated responses (n=12 for West Bengal and n=5 for Bangladesh) where consumers have used these brands at least six months earlier and have presently switched over to different brands. Respondents from both West Bengal and Bangladesh were selected conveniently from urban milieus. From West Bengal, participants belonged to urban conglomerates, namely, Kolkata (n=117), Asansol (n=66), Burdwan (n=49), Durgapur (n=31), Chandannagar (n=18) and Siliguri (n=14). From Bangladesh, responses were obtained from cities of Dhaka (n=73), Chittagong (n=62), Khulna (n=41), Gazipur (n=34), Barishal (n=25), Cumilla (n=19), Sylhet (n=19) and Rangpur (n=14). A complete picture of the demographic profile of the respondents in both West Bengal and Bangladesh has been portrayed in Table 5.

Table 5: Demographic Profile of Respondents Surveyed in West Bengal and Bangladesh

Component		West Bengal		Bangladesh	
		Frequency	Percent	Frequency	Percent
Gender	Male	146	49.5	144	50.2
	Female	149	50.5	143	49.8
	TOTAL	295	100.0	287	100.0
Age	Below 18	26	8.8	12	4.2
	18-25	59	20.0	44	15.3
	26-35	117	39.7	132	46.0
	36-50	73	24.7	62	21.6
	Above 50	20	6.8	37	12.9
	TOTAL	295	100.0	287	100.0
Occupation	Student	36	12.2	42	14.6
	Salaried (Government Service)	87	29.5	69	24.0
	Salaried (Private Service)	74	25.1	81	28.2
	Businessperson/ Self-Employed	69	23.4	62	21.6
	Professional	29	9.8	33	11.5
	TOTAL	295	100.0	287	100.0
Smartphone Used	Samsung	128	43.4	134	46.7
	Xiaomi	167	56.6	153	53.3
	TOTAL	295	100.0	287	100.0

Analysis and Discussion

The information obtained in the context of the current study suggests that marked divergences exist in terms of the cultural background and the purchase behaviours demonstrated by the study participants in West Bengal and Bangladesh.

Cultural Dimensions

Respondents in the two adjoining regions also exhibited distinct perceptual variances towards the personality of the Samsung and Xiaomi smartphone brands. The region-centric comparison in the context of the various cultural dimensions has been represented in Table 6. The items in the scale have been calculated on a traditional 5-point Likert scale ranging from "1" (Strongly Agree) to "5" (Strongly Disagree) since they only represent a fragment of the underlying perceptual repertoire and focus on mild degrees of consensus, thereby reducing fatigue and not representing those at the extremes (Leung, 2011).

Table 6: Comparing Hofstede's Cultural Dimensions among Respondents in West Bengal & Bangladesh

Variables in the Hofstede's Framework	West Bengal		Bangladesh	
	Mean	S.D.	Mean	S.D.
Power Distance Index (PDI)	3.35	0.91	2.11	1.00
Uncertainty Avoidance Index (UAI)	3.52	1.12	3.58	1.21
Individualism vs Collectivism (IVC)	2.17	1.16	2.09	1.06
Masculinity vs Femininity (MVF)	3.23	0.80	2.38	0.84
Long-Term vs Short-Term Orientation (LSO)	3.69	1.22	3.87	1.08
Indulgence vs Restraint (IVR)	3.04	0.84	2.32	1.08

As observed in Table 4, Bangladesh scores higher ($\bar{x}=2.11$) than West Bengal ($\bar{x}=3.35$) in terms of the "Power Distance" dimension ($\bar{x}=2.11$). It may be understood from the results that the respondents in Bangladesh tend to acknowledge and presume that the dynamics of power and income, to a certain extent, are disseminated in a lopsided manner in their society. This is relative to their counterparts in West Bengal, where respondents have generally expressed their indifference to the same parameter. While it is posited that no two societies can be replicas of each other, in the context of the current study, the dimensions of power and inequality are more unevenly distributed in Bangladesh than in West Bengal.

At this point, it must also be mentioned that the association of the items in the dimension is typically statistical in nature instead of being absolute (Hofstede, 2011). In terms of the cultural dimension of "Uncertainty Avoidance", both West Bengal ($\bar{x}=3.52$) and Bangladesh have fared similarly ($\bar{x}=3.58$), and their scores imply that they have relatively lower degrees of tolerance for ambiguity. Although there is a little deviation in terms of the mean scores of the two regions, it would be unfair to state that Bangladesh fares weaker than West Bengal in terms of the Uncertainty Avoidance Index. Respondents across both cultures have been conditioned to experience comfort or discomfort in amorphous milieus that tend to present unorthodox and uncharted consequences. Both cultures are known to possess austere behavioural stipulations that shape their ability to mitigate the likelihoods of occurrence of such ambiguous circumstances under stringent regulations and legal conditions, as well as discontentment concerning aberrant views. In terms of the "Individualism vs Collectivism" parameter, both cultures are largely "collectivist" in nature. For the sake of comparison, Bangladesh ($\bar{x}=2.09$) exhibits a more collectivist culture than West Bengal ($\bar{x}=2.17$), based on the mean scores, implying that the respondents dwell in a society that is generally assimilated into groups.

In other words, people in both cultures (with Bangladesh at an advantage) do not prefer to care for themselves and their immediate family members merely. However, they encompass individuals who, despite the trend of familial disintegration into nuclear units of late, have been typically conditioned from an early age to cohabitate and take care of persuasive, staunch and cohesive extended families. Such units, archetypally comprising of grandparents and other kith and kin, are typified as individuals who shower their blessings and safeguard all family members unconditionally, for the wholehearted loyalty doled out to them. Again, Bangladesh is more "masculine" as a society ($\bar{x}=2.38$) when compared to West Bengal ($\bar{x}=3.23$). Women in West Bengal, which has been perceived as a relatively more "feminine" society, possesses unpretentious and considerate value structures, much like their male counterparts. However, in Bangladesh, which is perceived largely as a "masculine" society, women also express self-assuredness and competitiveness to a certain degree, in contrast to the male members. There is a discernible disproportion between the value frameworks across both genders in the Bangladeshi culture compared to West Bengal. There may even be a reference to fundamental values that may remain below the level of consciousness or may be too embarrassing or agonizing to be deliberated upon unambiguously. When the two cultures are compared in terms of their "Long-term vs Short-term Orientation", respondents in both West Bengal ($\bar{x}=3.69$) and Bangladesh ($\bar{x}=3.87$) agree that their respective cultures possess a "short-term" approach, given that they prefer to emphasize on the present-day or former states of affairs and reckon them to be more crucial than the future.

Here again, the mean scores demonstrate marginal deviation, although the Bangladeshi culture is more "short-term oriented" than that of West Bengal, merely for comparison. Respondents in both cultures attach immense significance to the fulfilment of social agreements and compliance with established customs, norms, traditions and prevailing social hierarchies. Finally, when the two cultures are compared, in light of the "Indulgence vs Restraint" parameter, West Bengal ($\bar{x}=3.04$) scores fairly higher in comparison to Bangladesh ($\bar{x}=2.32$), suggesting more "indulgence" than "restraint" on the members of the society. This indicates that respondents in West Bengal dwell in a societal milieu that consents to moderately emotional gratification of their rudimentary and innate desires associated with relishing life and deriving pleasure. In contrast, the gratification of individual needs is moderately controlled through stringent social norms in the culture of Bangladesh. In summary, it is clear that considerable divergences exist between the cultures of West Bengal and Bangladesh in terms of the specific dimensions of "Power Distance", "Masculinity vs Femininity", and "Indulgence and Restraint."

Brand Personality Dimensions

As evidenced above, there are apparent differences in the cultural dimensions between people in West Bengal and Bangladesh. The subsequent proposition that has been investigated is whether and how such cultural parameters impact how the respondents perceive the personality traits of the two smartphone brands (Samsung and Xiaomi) considered in the current study. In other words, the study has attempted to establish whether respondents in West Bengal and Bangladesh view the personality traits of the Samsung and Xiaomi brand contrarily. Multiple regression was conducted to determine the impact of the various cultural dimensions on the various personality items of the smartphone brands for both regions. The results have been summarized in Table 7.

Table 7: Multiple Regression Results of Brand Personality Items and Cultural Dimensions

Dimensions/ Items	West Bengal						Bangladesh					
	Samsung (128)			Xiaomi (167)			Samsung (134)			Xiaomi (153)		
	β	R^2	Sig.	β	R^2	Sig.	β	R^2	Sig.	β	R^2	Sig.
Brand Personality Dimensions/ Items												
Responsibility		p=0.031*			p=0.382			p=0.527			p=0.015*	
Down-to-earth	0.140	0.961	0.000*	0.286	0.872	0.121	0.172	0.780	0.008*	0.122	0.972	0.433
Stable	0.144	0.920	0.001*	0.548	0.723	0.040*	0.093	0.771	0.215	0.095	0.983	0.000*
Responsible	0.300	0.911	0.074	0.420	0.627	0.000*	0.048	0.709	0.203	0.194	0.840	0.026*
Activity		p=0.031*			p=0.011*			p=0.009*			p=0.423	
Active	0.019	0.734	0.000*	0.031	0.960	0.047*	0.270	0.751	0.013*	0.161	0.817	0.782
Dynamic	0.223	0.883	0.631	0.049	0.867	0.393	0.266	0.628	0.015*	0.030	0.827	0.000*
Innovative	0.403	0.862	0.010*	0.013	0.717	0.022*	0.234	0.907	0.339	0.094	0.798	0.048*
Aggressiveness		p=0.423			p=0.026*			p=0.025*			p=0.331	
Aggressive	0.011	0.911	0.004*	0.154	0.676	0.035*	0.236	0.893	0.212	0.148	0.757	0.468
Bold	0.020	0.853	0.000*	0.266	0.901	0.000*	0.289	0.783	0.000*	0.145	0.947	0.328
Stability		p=0.007*			p=0.544			p=0.429			p=0.238	
Ordinary	0.226	0.837	0.129	0.137	0.831	0.140	0.118	0.642	0.063	0.213	0.751	0.000*
Simple	0.258	0.843	0.006*	0.196	0.873	0.722	0.034	0.659	0.005*	0.192	0.910	0.304
Emotionality		p=0.338			p=0.421			p=0.524			p=0.021*	
Romantic	0.246	0.835	0.085	0.202	0.677	0.033*	0.080	0.975	0.440	0.114	0.662	0.000*
Sentimental	0.041	0.793	0.694	0.092	0.772	0.103	0.147	0.632	0.022*	0.078	0.786	0.001*
Significance of Linear Regression		p=0.007*			p=0.014*			p=0.021*			p=0.139	
Cultural Dimensions												
PDI	0.231	0.782	0.018*	0.391	0.929	0.292	0.122	0.830	0.024*	0.177	0.892	0.003*
UAI	0.031	0.810	0.024*	0.135	0.849	0.048*	0.192	0.725	0.000*	0.065	0.728	0.000*
IVC	0.024	0.922	0.311	0.072	0.853	0.320	0.085	0.765	0.035*	0.148	0.713	0.492
MVF	0.412	0.953	0.139	0.208	0.908	0.000*	0.250	0.639	0.193	0.289	0.692	0.526
LSO	0.239	0.924	0.000*	0.367	0.861	0.023*	0.163	0.620	0.235	0.015	0.872	0.007*
IVR	0.012	0.896	0.089	0.133	0.681	0.000*	0.263	0.886	0.007*	0.243	0.852	0.013*
Significance of Linear Regression		p=0.002*			p=0.008*			p=0.015*			p=0.102	

*significant at the 5 per cent level

It is clear from Table 6 that respondents in Bangladesh and West Bengal perceive the personality of Samsung and Xiaomi divergently. For instance, the Samsung brand in West Bengal was observed to be down-to-earth, stable, active, innovative, aggressive, bold and simple, as they were significant at the 5 per cent level. Contrastingly, for Bangladesh, personality traits such as down-to-earth, active, dynamic, bold, simple and sentimental were significant at the 5 per cent level. Four personality items, namely, down-to-earth, active, bold, and simple, were commonly attributed to the Samsung brand in both cultures (33 per cent commonality). Attributes such as sentimental and dynamic were far from significant for the Samsung brand in West Bengal, while the romantic and innovative personality traits of Samsung barely exhibited any significance in the context of Bangladesh.

For Xiaomi in West Bengal, only seven personality traits were found to be significant, namely, stable, responsible, active, innovative, aggressive, bold and romantic. Even in Bangladesh, seven traits proved to be significant: stable, responsible, dynamic, innovative, ordinary, romantic, and sentimental. The only commonly perceived traits in both cultures were stable, responsible, innovative and romantic. As in the case of the Samsung brand, the degree of commonality was 33 per cent. Brand personality traits such as dynamic and straightforward were not significant in West Bengal, while five traits, namely active, aggressive, down-to-earth, bold and simple, were barely significant in Bangladesh. Apparent differences exist in how the brands are perceived across the two cultures, despite the multiple similarities.

Thus, the corresponding question arises whether the dimensions of culture as a specific construct play any role in the perception of brand personalities in the two regions. The significance values have been considered to investigate the versatile associations between people's perception towards brand personality dimensions (dependent variable) and the various cultural dimensions (predictor variables). For instance, for the Samsung smartphone brand in the case of West Bengal, the cultural dimensions of "Long-Term vs Short Term Orientation" (β-value: 0.239; explaining 92.4 per cent of the variance) and "Power Distance Index" (β-value: 0.231; explaining 78.2 per cent of the variance) had the greatest significant impact on the perceptual inferences towards the personality dimensions. In terms of predicting the personality items, "innovative" and "simple" accounted for the highest amount of variation for the Samsung brand in West Bengal, explaining 86.2 per cent and 84.3 per cent of the variance proportion respectively by the various cultural dimensions. In contrast, for Bangladesh, the cultural dimensions of "Indulgence vs Restraint" (β-value: 0.263; explaining 88.6 per cent of the variance) and "Power Distance Index" (β-value: 0.122; explaining 83 per cent of the variance) were most significant in predicting the impact on the personality items of the Samsung brand such as "bold", "active" and "dynamic", which accounted for the highest variance (78.3 per cent, 75.1 per cent and 62.8 per cent respectively).

As observed from Table 4, West Bengal tends to have a relatively "short-term" approach, wherein individuals prefer to dwell in the present moment and value immediate results while striving to establish parity with their peers and other acquaintances. Hence, being "innovative" for any given brand is a key to survive and maintain a competitive advantage in the given cultural setting. People would naturally prefer smartphone brands that offer more practical value as opposed to aesthetic appeal. More importantly, the fact that West Bengal scores relatively lower than Bangladesh in terms of "power distance" cannot be discounted. Coupled with the "short-term" orientation of respondents, individuals demonstrate an inclination to approve of equality and parity, of course, concerning Bangladesh. Due to the more minor discrepancies in terms of salary structures and status, they would crave brands that convey "simplicity".

In contrast, it may be noted that Bangladesh has a relatively lower beta coefficient (β-value: 0.034), explaining lesser potency of the impact of the cultural variables on the personality dimensions. In the case of Samsung smartphone brands in West Bengal, consumers seek order and a well-defined arrangement of apt cultural and national symbols, as they perceive in the case of Samsung. For Bangladesh, it is observed that they dwell in a society where "restraint" is on the higher side, and more importantly, they score higher in terms of "power distance" as well, compared to West Bengal. Individuals in Bangladesh are conditioned by their belief systems guided by stringent societal norms and practices, and favourable emotions are communicated in a relatively less accessible manner. People in such a culture place less importance on individual control and freedom. Moreover, even the power dynamics are biased in favour of people occupying positions of power, as they are respected more and perceived to possess intrinsic traits that trigger better decision-making capacities. It is not unusual to see greater significance being cast on personality items such as "bold" (explaining 78.3 per cent variation), "active" (75.1 per cent variation) and "dynamic" (62.8 per cent variation).

Again, in the case of West Bengal, the cultural dimensions of "Long-Term vs Short-Term Orientation" (β-value: 0.548; explaining 86.1 per cent of the variance), followed by "Masculinity vs Femininity" (β-value: 0.208; explaining 90.8 per cent of the variance) were observed to have the highest significant impact on the perceptions towards brand personality items concerning Xiaomi. In contrast, "Indulgence vs Restraint" (β-value: 0.243; explaining 85.2 per cent of the variance) followed by "Power Distance Index" (β-value: 0.177; explaining 89.2 per cent of the variance) accounted for the highest amount of impact on the perceptions towards the brand personality of Xiaomi in Bangladesh. The personality items that had the greatest significant impact due to the cultural dimensions in West Bengal (for Xiaomi) were "stable" (explaining 72.3 per cent variation), "responsible" (62.7 per cent) and "bold" (60.1 per cent). Based on the scores, West Bengal possesses a "feminine" type of culture, typified by features such as affectionate and considerate towards others, gentleness and the joy obtained from the more minor things in life. West Bengal scores higher on the feminine count, which happens to be in sync with its low power distance score. This probably explains why respondents have preferred stability and responsibility as prime traits they find in their usage of the Xiaomi brand. As people in West Bengal prefer to communicate about power directly, the Xiaomi brand manufacturers need to focus on key technical specifications and communicate them directly to their target group of consumers and develop their perceptions regarding the product. This illustrates why the individual personality traits of consumers rub off on the brand, and it is perceived as bold in West Bengal.

In contrast, Bangladesh accounted for items such as "ordinary" (84 per cent) and "responsible" (75.1 per cent), in the case of the Xiaomi brand. However, it was observed that culture did not significantly impact the overall perceptions of the personality items in the context of Bangladesh for the Xiaomi brand (insignificant at the 5 per cent level). In other words, it may be stated that culture, as a construct in Bangladesh, does not play any role in successfully predicting how the personality traits of the Xiaomi brand are perceived.

In summary, it may be stated that the cultural dimensions have a significant influence on how the Samsung smart phone brand is perceived in West Bengal and Bangladesh. However, the cultural dimensions have been observed to significantly influence the cultural dimensions (not items) of "responsibility", "activity", and "stability" in West Bengal, while they have significantly influenced "responsibility" and "aggressiveness" dimensions in Bangladesh. Similarly, for the Xiaomi brand, the cultural dimensions have significantly influenced the dimensions of "responsibility" and "aggressiveness" in West Bengal, while in Bangladesh, culture did not have any overall significant impact on the personality dimensions or traits.

Conclusion

The findings are consistent with the traits derived by the cross-cultural study conducted by Li et al.(2019). Parallels have also been detected with the study results conducted by Foscht et al. -(2008b), which discernibly substantiate the perceptual divergences of the "brand personality" construct in a cross-cultural context. Regardless of the indistinguishable positioning of the brand in the various cultural backdrops, clear differences were observed in terms of which the personality of the brand was perceived. In terms of mean score comparisons and variances, real divergences exist in the cultural perceptions by the consumer segments in the two adjoining cultures of West Bengal and Bangladesh. Samsung is perceived across both cultures as a responsible and trustworthy brand. It must be noted that "responsibility", in this context, does not necessarily refer to the social responsibility of a firm. It simply refers to the fact that the brand is perceived across both cultures as a dependable brand known to fulfil its promises towards target customers. This implies that if Samsung is desirous of establishing a uniform perception of the brand's personality in West Bengal and Bangladesh, they must develop unique brand positioning strategies that accentuate the attributes, thereby enabling target consumers to perceive Samsung analogously.

As a specific case in point, Samsung exhibited remarkable amounts of responsibility in its attempt to retrieve its brand identity after it was censured heavily for its flagship model "Samsung Galaxy Note 7" overheating and combusting or blowing up in a flurry of dispersed incidents (Moynihan, 2017). This prompted the aviation authorities in the USA, along with other airline organizations, to issue high-ranking caveats while urging passengers not to switch on or charge the specific brand of smart phone during ongoing flight journeys (Golson, 2016), and eventually banning the smart phone at the airport entry points(DOT Press Release, 2016). Notwithstanding, Samsung displayed immense responsibility by accepting accountability for the unfortunate incident and not blaming the battery manufacturers (ET Editorials, 2017).

However, there are divergences in the manner in which the brand is perceived otherwise. For example, while West Bengal additionally perceives that "activity" and "stability" are personality dimensions that define the Samsung brand adequately, respondents in Bangladesh feel that "aggressiveness" is a trait that is better suited to defining the identity of the brand. The smart phone market in Bangladesh has become overly aggressive in the recent past, with increased competition being injected by Chinese smart phone companies. Even homegrown brands such as Symphony have experienced condensed market shares, making the market for smart phones in Bangladesh extremely volatile. Consumers have found the Samsung brand to be bold and assertive in its communication strategies. Samsung has evolved as the market leader in the smart phone market of Bangladesh for the first time(StatCounter, 2019), with its sales volume witnessing a YoY surge of 203 percent in 2019(Choudhary, 2019). Moreover, consumers have borne testimony to an array of new models of Samsung smartphones in the last couple of years in response to the competition along with optimizations in terms of local assembly and manufacturing. Moreover, consumers in Bangladesh also witnessed the domination of Samsung in their respective price brands in terms of their diversified portfolio of smartphone models. For instance, for every Samsung Galaxy J series of smart phones released at the lower end of the price spectrum, there is a Galaxy A and Galaxy Z series targeted to the mid-range and upscale consumers, with relatively more pricey features and materials.

The cultural dimension of "Power Distance Index" is observed as a common cultural dimension, influencing the perceptions of brand personalities in both the regions, although, Bangladesh has a higher PDI than West Bengal. Moreover, in West Bengal, the relatively "Short-Term" cultural perspective has also played a key role in shaping the perception of the Samsung brand personality as "stable", "active" and "responsible". The marketing communications as well as promotional strategies of Samsung have been tailored into traditional arrangements. It may be expected that Samsung attempts to reach out to a wide array of target audiences in West Bengal, especially to the middle-income segment, who are known to confer with their peers and acquaintances, the product benefits and other attributes, before arriving at a consent relating to purchase. It is crucial that Samsung endeavours to promote the tangible and intangible social benefits of their offerings more to their target customers, in order to make their decision-making process simpler. Bangladesh has also scored higher than West Bengal in terms of "restraint". Accordingly, customers of Samsung in Bangladesh must be au fait with not merely the social paybacks of the smart phones, but also get detailed insights relating to their practicality and how they fit into the prevailing social structure.

In the case of the Xiaomi brand, consumers in West Bengal found the personality traits "active" and "aggressive" to be appropriate in defining the brand, while those in Bangladesh perceived it to be possessing more of a "responsible" and "emotional" brand personality. The cultural parameters that were significant in predicting the personality dimensions in West Bengal were found to be "short-term orientation", "femininity", and "indulgence". Since West Bengal scores lower than Bangladesh in terms of masculinity, it may be regarded generally as a feminine culture. Xiaomi, a Chinese smart phone major, can use a polycentric approach to appeal to both men and women neutrally. In other words, respondents in West Bengal learn about products and their attributes under peer-centric conversations, conciliation, and arriving at a consensus.

Given that the brand is perceived to possess a "responsible" personality, it is clear that Xiaomi focuses on releasing its products by adopting a collaborative model that requires inputs from customer levels. It is one of the prime reasons why Xiaomi has become a global name in the mid-market smart phone segment. The company is known to take immense care of their customers' experiences, using crowdsourcing as a critical instrument. The company intends to learn about continually improving its product offerings by using cocreation as an implement, wherein they connect with their target customers through an indigenous platform called "MIUI forum". It justifies why the brand is typically perceived as responsible in the context of West Bengal.

The brand is aggressive to the extent of its pricing. It is also known to use the 'flash sale' concept online quite frequently, thereby pushing demand for the product. It competes at neck-to-neck margins with lower-range smartphone brands such as Lenovo and Samsung, to name a few, which makes it an aggressive brand. However, it must be remembered that aggression and responsibility coupled together triggers positive connotations, as they choose not to compromise with quality by using second-rate materials (ET Bureau, 2019). In Bangladesh, however, the impacting cultural dimensions are observed to be "restraint" and "higher power distance", but it does not impact the perception of brand personality dimensions. However, the individual dimensions that have a significant bearing are "responsible" and "emotionality". Due to the insignificant impact, it cannot be stated with confidence that culture has any role in shaping people's perceptions of the Xiaomi brand of smartphones in Bangladesh. However, it must be noted that "responsibility" is commonly perceived across both cultures otherwise.

Managerial Implications

The current study is unique in that it offers a new-fangled perspective to looking at cross-cultural research. For instance, it would not be an oddity to conduct the study in the context of Bangladesh and India, as they are established nations with autonomously functioning governments. However, the current study provides a breakthrough in establishing that cross-cultural studies can also be conducted in the context of two regions, which belong to different countries but share common cultures. The study first establishes how brand personalities are perceived differently due to cultural divergences that persist in the two aforementioned political regions. It is evident from the study results that significant differences exist in the manner in which the brand personality of the smart phones is perceived across the two adjacent regions of West Bengal and Bangladesh.

The study offers valuable insights into the fact that Samsung and Xiaomi, despite being global brands and positioned analogously in both the regions (and all other major global markets), there exist clear differences in the perceptions towards brand personality. It provides meaningful lessons to the global smart phone companies' brand managers to emphasise the identified personality traits. Further, detailed insights into the cultural dimensions can help marketing practitioners to improve their communications and promotional strategies and better connect with their target customers in the respective regions. Since there exists no infallible approach to utilize cultural diversity as an implement to drive marketing communications efficaciously, smartphone brands can make efforts to localize their promotions, which albeit pricey, can prove to be effective. The other alternative is for smartphone brands to risk the germination of incoherent brands. It is also important to note that smartphone manufacturers need not find it necessary to transform their overall identity across the regions they are operating in but develop an enhanced comprehension of the cultural divergences and traditions, norms, and practices of the counties smartphone brands are targeted. The study furnishes adequate evidence to support the fact that smartphone brands are highly likely to pay off if they consider culture when designing and implementing their marketing communications programs.

Marketers must investigate the most effective manner of determining when and where along the customer journey. It would be apt to acclimatize their tailored marketing communication programs to specific markets. The key is to shape, run-through and acquire an effective brand personality, brand imagery and other anthropomorphic elements to evaluate the differences in effectiveness in such promotional avenues. The study shall offer branding professionals practical insights in building stronger and more unique personalities for their brands to nurture more robust relationships with their target customers whilst staying true to their brand. More often than not, marketers of global brands tend to blend the line in terms of West Bengal and Bangladesh's cultural dimensions due to shared languages, mutual respect and admiration for art and literature, and other such socio-cultural similarities. The study demonstrates that despite such similarities, there are noteworthy divergences in how the two cultures are oriented and how they impact how perceptions are shaped. It further establishes the idea that instead of smart phone brands endeavouring to establish commonalities in brand personality traits and dimensions across culturally analogous regions, they must appreciate the divergences in terms of respondents' perception in the respective cultures. This would help the brands develop more robust and unique personalities. For instance, the Samsung brand is perceived as an "emotional" brand in both the regions of West Bengal and Bangladesh, and it is established in the study that cultural dimensions play a key role in significantly shaping such perceptions towards the said brand.

Hence, the company can shift its focus from developing the smart phone brand with "romantic" or "sentimental" traits and focus on, say, "responsibility", which is commonly perceived across both cultures. More importantly, the manufacturers can focus on positioning the Samsung brand with an "active" personality in West Bengal while maintaining an "aggressive" personality in Bangladesh, given its current market dynamics. Similarly, Xiaomi, a disruptive Chinese smart phone manufacturer, especially in the Indian and Bangladesh markets, can focus on positioning the brand as "aggressive" in West Bengal instead of focussing on building it as a "stable" or "emotional" brand yet. Simply put, such smartphone majors can prefer to accentuate a personality attribute that is sought-after in a specific region/ market, but not inevitably in the context of other regions/ markets. This would essentially help them shape their brand as more pertinent and acceptable to the people in the said region, in that they would be able to construct a better idea of themselves (or personalities) from the prevailing beliefs about themselves, coupled with the feedbacks derived from others. This is notwithstanding that an incompatible brand image might crop up, even if the personalities are uniquely identified. This is critical, especially in today's era of globalization, where global brands strive to achieve scale efficiencies by focussing on standardization more than differentiation. However, since the brands are highly market-centric in their approach, the idea is to position the brand differently and cleverly by communicating different personality traits that are more appropriate in the said culture. For instance, Samsung has been an established player in the smart phone market of West Bengal, and given its wide array of products in the market, it is generally perceived as a "stable" brand, mostly because people have a relatively lower score on power distance spectrum and they generally possess a short-term cultural orientation. Keeping this view in mind, Samsung can focus on developing more female-centric models to target women buyers in West Bengal, and even for that matter, in India.

This is primarily of significance to brand marketers in the region because Samsung is typically perceived globally as a masculine brand (Matyszczyk, 2014). Interestingly, given the low power distance score in West Bengal, a strong marketing communications programme of Samsung with a female orientation might work well with male respondents unless marketed exclusively. Further, brand manufacturers must be careful not to price their products such that they become unaffordable. In such cultures like West Bengal, it would be a good idea for brand manufacturers to market their offerings by using noteworthy opinion leaders, which helps cement the brand's personality in the minds of the target audiences quite effectively. Brands that encourage consumers to value personal realization, and help them pursue activities that foster creativity and self-actualisation, often become successful in such cultures. However, before developing the personality traits and the brand's identity, a key question for marketers to probe into is whether or not such deliberations shall prove to be of any consequence in the long-term and whether such strategies would be cost-effective and practicable.

Limitations and Future Scope

Cross-cultural studies, inherently, are subject to their limitations and constraints. Although the current study attempts to bring about a new perspective to cross-cultural research by comparing politico-administrative units instead of countries at large, it is bound by multiple imperfections. For instance, the sample size is far too less to make more detailed and generalized comments on individuals' perceptions regarding the brand personality dimensions of smartphones. Larger sample sizes increase the confidence of making more informed decisions about the populations under consideration. One of the other issues faced in the current study was nationality bias, especially in Xiaomi smartphones in Bangladesh. Although adequate care has been taken to eliminate the "made-in image" of the Chinese smartphones, it was observed that respondents generally biased towards the product quality, brand acquaintance and their overall perceptions towards the personality of the said brand. The study can be expanded to determine the differences in the perception of brand personality among the SAARC countries and whether the respective cultures have any role in influencing such perceptions.

Further, the study makes use of the BPS developed by Geuens et al. (2009), which is an improvement over the seminal scale developed by J. L. Aaker (1997), may still not be considered as a universally accepted scale that appropriately defines brand personality (George & Anandkumar, 2012, 2018). Hence, further studies may be required to validate the selected countries' scale if the new BPS is considered. Alternatively, new measures may be developed to assess the dimensions of brand personality in the context of multiple brands.

References

Aaker, D. A. (1991). Managing brand equity : capitalizing on the value of a brand name. Free Press.

Aaker, J. L. (1997). Dimensions of brand personality. Journal of Marketing Research, 34(3), 347–356. https://doi.org/10.2307/3151897

Åberg, L. (2015). Co-creating A Brand Personality-An empirical case study on how a firm personifies its own brand by collaborating with other enterprises at the market. Uppsala University.

Ahmad, A., & Thyagaraj, K. S. (2015a). (PDF) Impact of Brand Personality on Brand Equity: The Role of Brand Trust, Brand Attachment, and Brand Commitment. Indian Journal of Marketing, 45(5), 14–26. https://doi.org/10.17010/ijom/2015/v45/i5/79937

Ahmad, A., & Thyagaraj, K. S. (2015b). Understanding the Influence of Brand Personality on Consumer Behavior. Journal of Advanced Management Science, 3(1), 38–43. https://doi.org/10.12720/joams.3.1.38-43

Ahmed, M., & Jan, M. T. (2015). An extension of Aaker's brand personality model from Islamic perspective: a conceptual study. Journal of Islamic Marketing, 6(3), 388–405. https://doi.org/10.1108/JIMA-10-2014-0068

Ajilore, K., & Solo-Anaeto, M. (2016). Smartphone Brand Personality as a Predictor of Brand Value among Undergraduates of Babcock University. Global Journal of Management and Business Research: E Marketing, 16(1), 32–41. https://globaljournals.org/item/5787-smartphone-brand-personality-as-a-predictor-of-brand-value-among-undergraduates-of-babcock-university

Alpatova, A., & Dall'Olmo, F. (2011). Comparing Brand Personality Measures. Academy of Marketing Conference 2011: Marketing Fields Forever, I

Ambroise, L., Ferrandi, J.-M., Merunka, D., & Valette-Florence, P. (2004). How well does brand personality predict brand choice ? In Asia Pacific Advances in Consumer Research. https://halshs.archives-ouvertes.fr/halshs-00525048

Anggraenia, A., & Rachmanita. (2015). Effects of Brand Love, Personality and Image on Word of Mouth; the Case of Local Fashion Brands among Young Consumers. In K. Pirzada (Ed.), Proceedings of the 2nd Global Conference on Business and Social Science-2015, Bali, Indonesia (pp. 442–447). Procedia - Social and Behavioral Sciences. https://doi.org/: 10.1016/j.sbspro.2015.11.058

Arsena, A., Silvera, D. H., & Pandelaere, M. (2014). Brand trait transference: When celebrity endorsers acquire brand personality traits. Journal of Business Research, 67(7), 1537–1543. https://doi.org/10.1016/j.jbusres.2014.01.011

Azoulay, A., & Kapferer, J.-N. (2003). Do brand personality scales really measure brand personality? Journal of Brand Management, 11(2), 143–155. https://doi.org/10.1057/palgrave.bm.2540162

Bairrada, C. M., Coelho, A., & Lizanets, V. (2019). The impact of brand personality on consumer behavior: the role of brand love. Journal of Fashion Marketing and Management, 23(1), 30–47. https://doi.org/10.1108/JFMM-07-2018-0091

Balachandran, P. K. (2006). Tracing the Sri Lanka-Kerala link - India. Hindustan Times. https://www.hindustantimes.com/india/tracing-the-sri-lanka-kerala-link/story YZCHbFMUS81hl7T1qAiB9N.html

Bayes, A. (2019, January 4). Cell-phone penetration and digital divide. The Financial Express. https://thefinancialexpress.com.bd/views/columns/cell-phone-penetration-and-digital-divide 1546617044

Becheur, I., Bayarassou, O., & Ghrib, H. (2017). Beyond Brand Personality: Building Consumer–Brand Emotional Relationship. Global Business Review, 18(3_suppl), S128–S144. https://doi.org/10.1177/0972150917693160

Beyers, J. (2017). Religion and culture: Revisiting a close relative. HTS Teologiese Studies / Theological Studies, 73(1), 1–9. https://doi.org/10.4102/hts.v73i1.3864

Bishnoi, V. K., & Kumar, A. (2016). Aaker's brand personality scale is not universal – Explanation and reasons for bikes in India. Journal of Marketing Analytics, 4(1), 14–27. https://doi.org/10.1057/jma.2016.3

Bozbay, Z., & Ozkan, E. (2016). The Effect of Brand Personality on Consumers' Brand Preference : The Mediating Role of Self-Expressive Value of Brand. In S. Erdoğan, D. Ç. Yildirim, & A. Gedikli (Eds.), International Congress of Management Economy and Policy (pp. 3536–3553). ICOMEP.

Buil, I., De Chernatony, L., & Martínez, E. (2012). Methodological issues in cross-cultural research: An overview and recommendations. In Journal of Targeting, Measurement and Analysis for Marketing (Vol. 20, Issues 3–4, pp. 223–234). Palgrave. https://doi.org/10.1057/jt.2012.18

Caprar, D. V., Devinney, T. M., Kirkman, B. L., & Caligiuri, P. (2015). Conceptualizing and measuring culture in international business and management: From challenges to potential solutions. In Journal of International Business Studies (Vol. 46, Issue 9, pp. 1011–1027). Palgrave Macmillan Ltd. https://doi.org/10.1057/jibs.2015.33

Cătălin, M. C., & Andreea, P. (2014). Brands as a Mean of Consumer Self-expression and Desired Personal Lifestyle. Procedia - Social and Behavioral Sciences, 109, 103–107. https://doi.org/10.1016/j.sbspro.2013.12.427

Cecere, G., Corrocher, N., & Battaglia, R. D. (2015). Innovation and competition in the smartphone industry: Is there a dominant design? Telecommunications Policy, 39(3–4), 162–175. https://doi.org/10.1016/j.telpol.2014.07.002

Chegini, F., Molan, S. B., & Kashanifar, S. S. (2016). An Examination of the Impact of Cultural Values on Brand Preferences in Tehran's Fashion Market. Procedia Economics and Finance, 36, 189–200. https://doi.org/10.1016/s2212-5671(16)30030-2

Chick, G. (1997). Cultural Complexity: The Concept and Its Measurement. Cross-Cultural Research, 31(4), 275–307. https://doi.org/10.1177/106939719703100401

Chordia, A. (2016). You'd Be Surprised To Know These Similarities Between India And Pakistan. Being Indian: Entertainment. http://www.beingindian.com/entertainment/similarities-between india-and-pakistan

Choudhary, A. (2019). Smartphone Market in Bangladesh Grew 45% YoY in Q1 2019 - Counterpoint Research. Counterpoint Research. https://www.counterpointresearch.com/smartphone-market bangladesh-grew-45-yoy-q1-2019/

Chovanová, H. H., Korshunov, A. I., & Babčanová, D. (2015). ScienceDirect Impact of Brand on Consumer Behavior. Procedia Economics and Finance, 34, 615–621. https://doi.org/10.1016/S2212-5671(15)01676-7

Chung, S., & Park, J. (2017). The influence of brand personality and relative brand identification on brand loyalty in the European mobile phone market. Canadian Journal of Administrative Sciences, 34, 47–62. https://doi.org/10.1002/CJAS.1321

Cronk, L. (2017). Culture's influence on behavior: Steps toward a theory. Evolutionary Behavioral Sciences, 11(1), 36–52. https://doi.org/10.1037/ebs0000069

Dheer, R. J., Lenartowicz, T., & Peterson, M. F. (2015). Mapping India's regional subcultures: Implications for international management. Journal of International Business Studies, 46, 443–467. https://doi.org/10.2307/43653760

DOT Press Release. (2016). DOT Bans All Samsung Galaxy Note7 Phones From Airplanes. Administration, United States Department of Transportation: Federal Aviation. https://www.faa.gov/news/updates/?newsId=86685

Ekinci, Y., & Hosany, S. (2006). Destination Personality: An Application of Brand Personality to Tourism Destinations. Journal of Travel Research, 45, 127–13. https://doi.org/10.1177/0047287506291603

Eringa, K., Caudron, L. N., Rieck, K., Xie, F., & Gerhardt, T. (2017). Research in Hospitality Management How relevant are Hofstede's dimensions for inter-cultural studies? A replication of Hofstede's research among current international business students. Research in Hospitality Management, 5(2), 187–198. https://doi.org/10.1080/22243534.2015.11828344

ET Bureau. (2019). Xiaomi India says can't make losses while pricing aggressively - The Economic Times. The Economic Times: Hardware. https://economictimes.indiatimes.com/tech/hardware/xiaomi-india-says-cant-make-losses-while-pricing-aggressively/articleshow/70286914.cms?from=mdr

ET Editorials. (2017). Samsung shows the way to protect a brand name. The Economic Times. https://economictimes.indiatimes.com/blogs/et-editorials/samsung-shows-the-way-to-protect-a-brand-name/

Fan, Y. (2000). A classification of Chinese culture. Cross Cultural Management: An International Journal, 7(2), 3–10. https://doi.org/10.1108/13527600010797057

Ford, C. S. (1942). Culture and Human Behavior. In The Scientific Monthly (Vol. 55, pp. 546–557). American Association for the Advancement of Science. https://doi.org/10.2307/17855

Foscht, T., Maloles, C., Swoboda, B., Morschett, D., & Sinha, I. (2008a). The impact of culture on brand perceptions: A six-nation study. Journal of Product & Brand Management, 17(3), 131–142. https://doi.org/10.1108/10610420810875052

Foscht, T., Maloles, C., Swoboda, B., Morschett, D., & Sinha, I. (2008b). The impact of culture on brand perceptions: A six-nation study. Journal of Product & Brand Management, 17(3), 131–142. https://doi.org/10.1108/10610420810875052

George, J., & Anandkumar, V. (2012). From Aaker to Heere: A Review and Comparison of Brand Personality Scales. SSRN Electronic Journal, 1(3), 30–52. https://doi.org/10.2139/ssrn.2061570

George, J., & Anandkumar, V. (2018). Dimensions of Product Brand Personality. Vision: The Journal of Business Perspective, 22(4), 377–386. https://doi.org/10.1177/0972262918803496

Geuens, M., Weijters, B., & De Wulf, K. (2009). A new measure of brand personality. International Journal of Research in Marketing, 26(2), 97–107. https://doi.org/10.1016/j.ijresmar.2008.12.002

Golson, J. (2016). The Galaxy Note 7 will be banned from all US airline flights - The Verge. The Verge. https://www.theverge.com/2016/10/14/13288978/samsung-galaxy-note-7-flight-ban-faa-us

Gondim Mariutti, F., & de Moura Engracia Giraldi, J. (2019). Country brand personality of Brazil: a hindsight of Aaker's theory. Place Branding and Public Diplomacy, 1–14. https://doi.org/10.1057/s41254-019-00153-3

Gorbaniuk, O., Sokolowski, T., Markowska, E., Czajka, K., & Mielczarek, A. (2015). Brand Personality and Consumer-Based Brand Equity: A Study among Polish Consumers. In Cultural Perspectives in a Global Marketplace. Developments in Marketing Science: Proceedings of the Academy of Marketing Science (pp. 88–93). Springer, Cham. https://doi.org/10.1007/978-3-319-18696-2_37

Hanel, P. H. P., Maio, G. R., Soares, A. K. S., Vione, K. C., de Holanda Coelho, G. L., Gouveia, V. V., Patil, A. C., Kamble, S. V., & Manstead, A. S. R. (2018). Cross-Cultural Differences and Similarities in Human Value Instantiation. Frontiers in Psychology, 9(MAY), 849. https://doi.org/10.3389/fpsyg.2018.00849

Hofstede, G. (1980). Culture's consequences : international differences in work-related values. Sage Publications.

Hofstede, G. (2011). Dimensionalizing Cultures: The Hofstede Model in Context. Online Readings in Psychology and Culture, 2(1), 1–26. https://doi.org/10.9707/2307-0919.1014

Hofstede, G., & Bond, M. H. (1984). Hofstede's Culture Dimensions. Journal of Cross-Cultural Psychology, 15(4), 417–433. https://doi.org/10.1177/0022002184015004003

Holt, D. (2010). Brands and Branding.

Hopes, D. (2014). Being objective: communities of practice and the use of cultural artefacts in digital learning environments [University of Birmingham]. In PQDT - UK & Ireland (Issue March). https:/login.pallas2.tcl.sc.edu/login?url=https://search.proquest.com/docview/1654748590?accounti d=13965%0Ahttp://resolver.ebscohost.com/openurl?ctx_ver=Z39.88 -2004&ctx_enc=info:ofi/enc:UTF-8&rfr_id=info:sid/ProQuest+Dissertations+%26+Theses+Global&rft_v

J. Karlin, N., & Weil, J. (2019). Exploring Cultural Similarity and Cultural Diversity: A Cross-National Study of Nine Countries. Journal of Aging Science, 07(02), 1–9. https://doi.org/10.35248/2329-8847.19.07.204

Jain, A. (2019). India Smartphone Shipments Reached a Record-High 49 Million units Defying the Economic Slowdown Trends in Other Sectors - Counterpoint Research. Counterpoint Research. https://www.counterpointresearch.com/india-smartphone-shipments-reached record-high-49-million-units-defying-economic-slowdown-trends-sectors/

Jansson, E. (2013). Cross-cultural differences in brand image perception-An exploration of the Volvo brand.

Jones, M. L. (2007). Hofstede - Culturally questionable? In Oxford Business & Economics Conference Proceedings. Oxford University. http://ro.uow.edu.au/commpapers/370

Kankaraš, M., & Moors, G. (2010). Researching measurement equivalence in cross-cultural studies. Psihologija, 43(2), 121–136. https://doi.org/10.2298/PSI1002121K

Kapferer, J.-N. (1996). 'Building Strong Brands.' Journal of Brand Management, 3(4), 278–280. https://doi.org/10.1057/bm.1996.8

Keller, K. L., & Richey, K. (2006). The importance of corporate brand personality traits to a successful 21st century business. Journal of Brand Management, 14(1–2), 74–81. https://doi.org/10.1057/palgrave.bm.2550055

Khandai, S., Agrawal, B., & Gulla, A. (2015). BRAND PERSONALITY SCALE: HOW DO INDIAN CONSUMERS INTERPRET THE PERSONALITY DIMENSIONS? In Asian Academy of Management Journal (Vol. 20, Issue 1).

Khandelwal, R. (2019). Global Smartphone Companies: An Overview. Market Realist. https://marketrealist.com/2019/09/global-smartphone-companies-an-overview/

Kim, C. K., Han, D., & Park, S.-B. (2001). The effect of brand personality and brand identification on brand loyalty: Applying the theory of social identification. Japanese Psychological Research, 43(4), 195–206. https://doi.org/10.1111/1468-5884.00177

Kumar, A. (2018). Story of Aaker's brand personality scale criticism. Spanish Journal of Marketing - ESIC, 22(2), 203–230. https://doi.org/10.1108/SJME-03-2018-005

Lee, J. A. (1966). Cultural analysis in overseas operations. The International Executive, 8(3), 5–6. https://doi.org/10.1002/tie.5060080303

Leung, S. O. (2011). A comparison of psychometric properties and normality in 4-, 5-, 6-, and 11 point likert scales. Journal of Social Service Research, 37(4), 412–421. https://doi.org/10.1080/01488376.2011.580697

Li, C., Li, D., Chiu, C.-Y., & Peng, S. (2019). Strong Brand From Consumers' Perspective: A Cross Cultural Study. Journal of Cross-Cultural Psychology, 50(1), 116–129. https://doi.org/10.1177/0022022118799456

Lindeberg, A., Blomkvist, C., & Johansson, M. (2012). Title: Understanding the relationship between Brand identity and Brand image-A case study of Coop Subject: Marketing Communication [Linnaeus University]. https://www.diva portal.org/smash/get/diva2:530562/FULLTEXT01.pdf

MacInnis, D. J., & Folkes, V. S. (2017). Humanizing brands: When brands seem to be like me, part of me, and in a relationship with me. Journal of Consumer Psychology, 27(3), 355–374. https://doi.org/10.1016/j.jcps.2016.12.003

Maehle, N., Otnes, C., & Supphellen, M. (2011). Consumers' perceptions of the dimensions of brand personality. Journal of Consumer Behaviour, 10(5), 290–303. https://doi.org/10.1002/cb.355

Malhotra, N. K., Agarwal, J., & Peterson, M. (1996). Methodological issues in cross-cultural marketing research: A state-of-the-art review. International Marketing Review, 13(5), 7–43. https://doi.org/10.1108/02651339610131379

Mason, K., & Batch, A. (2009). BrandLeveraging. Journal of Business, Industry and Economics, 13, 19–25.

Matyszczyk, C. (2014). Women prefer Apple, gentlemen prefer Samsung. CNET. https://www.cnet.com/news/women-prefer-apple-gentlemen-prefer-samsung/

Matzler, K., Strobl, A., Stokburger-Sauer, N., Bobovnicky, A., & Bauer, F. (2016). Brand personality and culture: The role of cultural differences on the impact of brand personality perceptions on tourists' visit intentions. Tourism Management, 52, 507–520. https://doi.org/10.1016/j.tourman.2015.07.017

McSweeney, B. (2002). Hofstede's Model of National Cultural Differences and their Consequences: A Triumph of Faith - a Failure of Analysis. Human Relations, 55(1), 89–118. https://doi.org/10.1177/0018726702551004

Milas, G., & Mlačić, B. (2007). Brand personality and human personality: Findings from ratings of familiar Croatian brands. Journal of Business Research, 60(6), 620–626. https://doi.org/10.1016/j.jbusres.2006.06.011

Moynihan, T. (2017). Samsung Finally Reveals Why the Galaxy Note 7 Kept Exploding | WIRED. The Wired. https://www.wired.com/2017/01/why-the-samsung-galaxy-note-7-kept exploding/

Muniz, K. M., & Marchetti, R. Z. (2012). Brand personality dimensions in the Brazilian context. BAR - Brazilian Administration Review, 9(2), 168–188. https://doi.org/10.1590/S1807 76922012000200004

Ngoc Anh, H. (2016). SMARTPHONE INDUSTRY: THE NEW ERA OF COMPETITION AND STRATEGY [Centria University of Applied Sciences]. https://www.theseus.fi/bitstream/handle/10024/119385/FinalthesisHNA.pdf?sequence=1&isAllowed=y

Norenzayan, A., Choi, I., & Nisbett, R. E. (2002). Cultural Similarities and Differences in Social and Social Psychology Bulletin, 28(1), 109–120.

Olsson, A., & Sandru, C. (2006). The Brand Proposition [Luleå University of Technology]. http://www.diva-portal.org/smash/get/diva2:1017610/FULLTEXT01.pdf

Overby, J. W., Woodruff, R. B., & Gardial, S. F. (2005). The influence of culture upon consumers' desired value perceptions: A research agenda. Marketing Theory, 5(2), 139–163. https://doi.org/10.1177/1470593105052468

Pandey, A. (2009). Understanding Consumer Perception of Brand Personality. The IUP Journal of Brand Management, 6(3, 4), 26–50. https://doi.org/10.2139/ssrn.1441824

Parks, J., & Tong, X. (2020). The impact of culture on brand personality: An empirical study of the lifestyle brands originating from the American South. Journal of Cultural Marketing Strategy, 4(2), 102–116. https://hstalks.com/article/5447/the-impact-of-culture-on-brand-personality-an-empi/

Paul, L., & Cornelia, C.-P. (2019). Plateauing at the peak The state of the smartphone. https://www2.deloitte.com/content/dam/Deloitte/uk/Documents/technology-media-telecommunications/deloitte-uk-plateauing-at-the-peak-the-state-of-the-smartphone.pdf

Pereira, R., C. Baranauskas, M. C., & Liu, K. (2015). On the relationships between norms, values and culture: Preliminary thoughts in HCI. IFIP Advances in Information and Communication Technology, 449, 30–40. https://doi.org/10.1007/978-3-319-16274-4_4

Phau, I., & Lau, K. C. (2000). Conceptualising brand personality: A review and research propositions. Journal of Targeting, Measurement and Analysis for Marketing, 9(1), 52–69. https://doi.org/10.1057/palgrave.jt.5740005

Press Trust of India. (2013, January 20). West Bengal witnesses 61% urban mobile penetration. Business Standard News. https://www.business-standard.com/article/economy-policy/west bengal-witnesses-61-urban-mobile-penetration-112032900006_1.html

Press Trust of India Report. (2020, November 6). Vivo India to raise localisation level to 40 pc by 2021. The Economic Times: Telecom. https://telecom.economictimes.indiatimes.com/news/vivo-india-to-raise-localisation-level-to-40-pc-by-2021/79082341

Puzakova, M., & Kwak, H. (2017). Should Anthropomorphized Brands Engage Customers? The Impact of Social Crowding on Brand Preferences. Journal of Marketing, 81(6), 99–115. https://doi.org/10.1509/jm.16.0211

Puzakova, M., Kwak, H., & Rocereto, J. (2009). ASSOCIATION FOR CONSUMER RESEARCH Pushing the Envelope of Brand and Personality: Antecedents and Moderators of Anthropomorphized Brands. In A. L. McGill & S. Shavitt (Eds.), Advances in Consumer Research (Vol. 36, pp. 413–420). Association for Consumer Research (ACR). http://www.copyright.com/.

Rahman, M., Bose, S., Babu, M. M., Dey, B. L., Roy, S. K., & Binsardi, B. (2019). Value Co-Creation as a Dialectical Process: Study in Bangladesh and Indian Province of West Bengal. Information Systems Frontiers, 21(3), 527–545. https://doi.org/10.1007/s10796-019-09902-4

Raj, P. (2020, November 7). Vivo India To Raise Level Of Localization In India To 40% By 2021. Next Big Brand. https://www.nextbigbrand.in/vivo-india-to-raise-level-of-localization-in india-to-40-by-2021/

Rajagopal, D. (2012). Interdependence of Personality Traits and Brand Identity in Measuring Brand Performance. In SSRN Electronic Journal (No. 20080-06-MKT). Elsevier BV. https://doi.org/10.2139/ssrn.1309864

Rajeswari, R., & Pirakatheeswari, P. (2014). A Study on Consumer Behaviour and Factors Influencing the Purchase Decision of Durable Goods with Reference to Salem District. International Research Journal of Business and Management, 7(2), 10–18. www.irjbm.org

Robertson, J., Lord Ferguson, S., Eriksson, T., & Näppä, A. (2019). The brand personality dimensions of business-to-business firms: a content analysis of employer reviews on social media. Journal of Business-to-Business Marketing, 26(2), 109–124. https://doi.org/10.1080/1051712X.2019.1603354

Roy, P., Khandeparkar, K., & Motiani, M. (2016). A lovable personality: The effect of brand personality on brand love. Journal of Brand Management, 23(5), 97–113. https://doi.org/10.1057/s41262-016-0005-5

Sathya, P., & Vijayasanthi, C. (2016). Consumer Behaviour towards Consumer Durable Goods in Thiruvarur District. International Journal of Science and Research, 5(5), 2319–7064. http://info.shine.com/Industry-

Sepora, T., Mahadi, T., & Jafari, S. M. (2012). Language and Culture. In International Journal of Humanities and Social Science (Vol. 2, Issue 17). www.ijhssnet.com

Shavitt, S., & Barnes, A. J. (2020). Culture and the Consumer Journey. Journal of Retailing, 96(1), 40–54. https://doi.org/10.1016/j.jretai.2019.11.009

Sheena, & Naresh, G. (2012). Do Brand Personalities Make a Difference to Consumers? Procedia - Social and Behavioral Sciences, 37, 31–37. https://doi.org/10.1016/j.sbspro.2012.03.272

Shen, T. (2017). Recognition of symbols in different cultures: Chinese culture vs. non-Chinese culture [Iowa State University]. https://lib.dr.iastate.edu/etd/15420

Shifat, S. A. (2020). The Smartphone Market Ecosystem of Bangladesh - DATABD.CO. https://databd.co/stories/the-smartphone-market-ecosystem-of-bangladesh-9830

Shyle, I., & Hysi, V. (2013). Brand personality as important element in creating strong brand equity. Proceedings of the 1st International Conference on "Research and Education – Challenges Towards the Future" (ICRAE2013), 24-25 May 2013, 24–25.

Silver, L. (2019, May 14). Smartphone Ownership Is Growing Rapidly Around the World, but Not Always Equally | Pew Research Center. Pew Research Center: Global Attitudes & Trends. https://www.pewresearch.org/global/2019/02/05/smartphone-ownership-is-growing-rapidly around-the-world-but-not-always-equally/

Srivastava, K., & Sharma, N. K. (2016). Consumer Perception of Brand Personality: An Empirical Evidence from India. Global Business Review, 17(2), 375–388. https://doi.org/10.1177/0972150915619814

Staplehurst, G., & Charoenwongse, S. (2012). Millward Brown: Point of View Why Brand Personality Matters. www.mb-blog.com.

StatCounter. (2019). Mobile Vendor Market Share Bangladesh | StatCounter Global Stats. Mobile Vendor Market Share Bangladesh Jan - Dec 2019. https://gs.statcounter.com/vendor-market share/mobile/bangladesh/2019

Su, J., & Tong, X. (2015). Brand personality and brand equity: Evidence from the sportswear industry. Journal of Product and Brand Management, 24(2), 124–133. https://doi.org/10.1108/JPBM-01-2014-0482

Sundar, A., & Noseworthy, T. J. (2016). Too Exciting to Fail, Too Sincere to Succeed: The Effects of Brand Personality on Sensory Disconfirmation. Journal of Consumer Research, 43(1), 44–67. https://doi.org/10.1093/jcr/ucw003

Sung, Y., Choi, S. M., Ahn, H., & Song, Y.-A. (2015). Dimensions of Luxury Brand Personality: Scale Development and Validation. Psychology & Marketing, 32(1), 121–132. https://doi.org/10.1002/mar.20767

Tessa, W. (2018). The Science Behind Branding and Consumer Choice. The Science Behind Branding and Consumer Choice. https://www.shutterstock.com/blog/science-branding-consumer-choice

Tomas, G., Hult, M., Ketchen, D. J., Griffith, D. A., Finnegan, C. A., Gonzalez-Padron, T., Harmancioglu, N., Huang, Y., Talay, B., & Cavusgil, S. T. (1995). Data equivalence in cross cultural international business research: assessment and guidelines. Management International Review, Journal of World Business, Strategic Management Journal and the Academy of Management Journal, 39, 1027–1044. https://doi.org/10.1057/palgrave.jibs.8400396

Triandis, H. C. (1989). The Self and Social Behavior in Differing Cultural Contexts. Psychological Review, 96(3), 506–520. https://doi.org/10.1037/0033-295X.96.3.506

Trimble, J. E. (2010). Cultural Measurement Equivalence. In C. S. Clauss-Ehlers (Ed.), Encyclopedia of Cross-Cultural School Psychology (pp. 316–318). Springer US. https://doi.org/10.1007/978-0-387-71799-9_112

Tunkkari, S. (2017). CULTURAL SIMILARITIES AND DIFFERENCES IN CONSUMER BEHAVIOUR Thesis CENTRIA UNIVERSITY OF APPLIED SCIENCES Business Management [Centria University of Applied Sciences]. https://www.theseus.fi/bitstream/handle/10024/125345/Tunkkari_Siobhan1.pdf?sequence=1

Usakli, A., & Baloglu, S. (2011). Brand personality of tourist destinations: An application of self-congruity theory. Tourism Management, 32(1), 114–127. https://doi.org/10.1016/j.tourman.2010.06.006

Vellnagel, C. C. (2020). Acquisition of the Role of Culture on the Relationship Between Brand Personality and Brand Desirability. In Cross-Cultural Brand Personality and Brand Desirability: An Empirical Approach to the Role of Culture on this Mediated Interplay (1st ed., Vol. 1, pp. 53–78). Gabler Verlag. https://doi.org/10.1007/978-3-658-31178-0_3

Wang, L., Doucet, L., & Northcraft, G. (2006). Culture, Affect, and Social Influence in Decision Making Groups. In Research on Managing Groups and Teams (Vol. 9, pp. 147–172). Emerald Group Publishing Limited. https://doi.org/10.1016/S1534-0856(06)09007-4

Williamson, D. (2002). Forward from a Critique of Hofstede's Model of National Culture. Human Relations, 55(11), 1373–1395. https://doi.org/10.1177/00187267025511006

Yasin, M., Porcu, L., Abusharbeh, M. T., & Liébana-Cabanillas, F. (2020). The impact of customer personality and online brand community engagement on intention to forward company and users generated content: Palestinian banking industry a case. Economic Research-Ekonomska Istraživanja, 33(1), 1985–2006. https://doi.org/10.1080/1331677X.2020.1752277

Zadeh, H. Z., & Rose, A. (2018). Impacts of culture on brand positioning and international marketing. International Journal of Academic Research and Development, 3(3), 82–86.

Zainuddin, M., Yasin, I. M., Arif, I., & Hamid, A. B. A. (2018). Alternative Cross-Cultural Theories: Why Still Hofstede? International Conference on Economics, Management and Social Study, December, 4–6. https://ssrn.com/abstract=3309633

Zainudin, M. I., Haji Hasan, F., & Othman, A. K. (2019). Halal brand personality and brand loyalty among millennial modest fashion consumers in Malaysia. Journal of Islamic Marketing, 11(6), 1277–1293. https://doi.org/10.1108/JIMA-10-2018-0187

Shaunak Roy is working as Assistant Professor, Faculty of Management, Department of Commerce and Management Studies, St. Xavier's College (Autonomous), Kolkata; Email: shaunak@sxccal.edu

Dr. Shivaji Banerjee former Head and Assistant Professor, Faculty of Management, Department of Commerce, St. Xavier's College (Autonomous), Kolkata; Email: drshivaji@sxccal.edu

Cost Efficiency Vis-à-Vis Revenue Efficiency Analysis of Indian Scheduled Commercial Banks in a Dynamic Environment

Aparna Bhatia
Assistant Professor, University School of Financial Studies,
Guru Nanak Dev University Amritsar

Megha Mahendru
Assistant Professor, Department of Commerce and Business Administration,
Khalsa College, Amritsar

Received 15 January 2021
Revised 10 March 2021
Accepted 12 April 2021

Abstract

The paper endeavours to analyze Cost Efficiency vis-à-vis Revenue Efficiency of Scheduled Commercial Banks (SCBs) as well as across ownership in India. Data Envelopment Analysis (DEA) has been employed to calculate the efficiency scores of SCBs over five points of time i.e. 2000-01, 2004-05, 2008-09, 2012-13 and 2016-17. The differences in the efficiency scores are examined by applying Analysis of Variance (ANOVA). The results of Cost and Revenue Efficiency of Indian Scheduled Commercial Banks highlight that the highest level of inefficiency subsist on the cost side as Scheduled Commercial Banks have higher Revenue Efficiency scores in comparison to Cost Efficiency scores. Cost Efficiency across ownership shows that Public Sector Banks have higher Cost Efficiency in 2000-01. Private Sector Banks are cost efficient in 2004-05 while Foreign Sector Banks show higher Cost Efficiency scores in 2008-09, 2012-13 and 2016-17. Revenue Efficiency scores shows that Public Sector Banks have higher scores as compared to Private and Foreign Sector Banks in the 2000-01 and 2004-05. Foreign Sector Banks are revenue efficient in 2008-09 and 2016-17 with Private Sector Banks taking the lead in 2012-13. The results of ANOVA reveal that there exists a statistically significant difference in Cost Efficiency and Revenue Efficiency among banks in different sectors over different points of time.

Keywords: Cost Efficiency, Revenue Efficiency, Scheduled Commercial Banks (SCBs), Data Envelopment Analysis, India.

Introduction

Efficiency refers to the best allocation of resources to obtain the highest level of outputs. It measures a bank's performance in relation to a yardstick at a given point of time (Ram Mohan and Ray 2004). The efficiency is associated with how a bank simultaneously minimizes cost and maximizes revenue, while operating on the frontier (Tandon *et al.*, 2003; Kumar, 2006 and Chatterjee *et al.*, 2014). Banks can take advantage of competitive environment only if these perform efficiently in the market (Bader *et al.*, 2008). If banks are fully efficient, these can have improved profitability which in turn provides safety to absorb huge risks (Berger et al, 1993 and Egesa, 2010). An efficient banking system helps to maintain financial stability in the economy and promotes economic growth (Rajan and Zingales, 1995; Levin, 1997; Cetorelli and Gambera, 2001; Egesa, 2010; Gulati, 2011b and Pančurová and Lyócsa, 2013). An efficient bank is able to provide more trustworthy services to the consumers at optimum prices. This helps to maintain faith, confidence and reliability of the customers in the banking sector (Zeitun and Benjelloun,

2013) which is the foundation of any service industry. Thus the efficiency of banking system is instrumental not only in the welfare of society but that of a country as a whole when it offers innovative and quality service at the minimum cost and simultaneously generates ample revenues towards country's GDP (Valverde*et al.*, 2003; Bader *et al.*, 2008 and Gulati and Kumar, 2011).

The literature on bank efficiency has expanded drastically since early nineties, and continues to flourish. Numerous studies have explored the efficiency performance of banks. The literature on efficiency of banks highlights that majority of the research articles have focused on Technical Efficiency i.e. reducing input to the maximum possible extent with given level of outputs or maximising the outputs with the given level of inputs. Technical Efficiency considers the ability of banks in using its inputs optimally or producing its outputs efficiently but it does not take into consideration their prices. Merely considering inputs-outputs will not provide any useful information as it will not lead banks to earn financial benefits unless and until their prices are also taken into consideration (Portela and Thanassoulis, 2007). Considering this research gap, the researchers shifted their focus on cost minimisation approach i.e.Cost Efficiency. Cost Efficiency assesses the relative performance of bank as against the best practice bank which is managing its operating costs at the lowest for producing the same output under similar technological conditions (Bader *et al.*, 2008 and Kamarudin*et al.*, 2014). Therefore, some studies exclusively concentrated on the Cost Efficiency aspect of the banks as Niazi (2003),Girardone*et al.* (2004), Das *et al.* (2005),Burki and Niazi (2006), Sahoo *et al.* (2007),Pasiouras and Kosimidou (2007), Ahmed (2008), Uddin and Suzuki (2011), Gulati (2011a), Kumar (2013) and Raina and Sharma (2013). The literature on banking that merely focuses on Cost Efficiency has been criticized for ignoring the Revenue Efficiency of banks because high cost incurring bank i.e. cost inefficient bank might be able to generate higher revenues than the cost efficient bank (Berger and Mester, 1997 and Berger and Humphrey, 1997). This is due to the reason that banks offer products and services through technology, which increases their cost and makes them temporarily cost inefficient but it might make them revenue efficient by boosting their turnover.Keeping in mind the revenue aspect, Ram Mohan and Ray (2004) exclusively reviewed the Revenue Efficiency performance of banks. Revenue Efficiency measures the comparative performance of bank as against the best practice bank which is producing the maximum output from the inputs available (Bader *et al.*, 2008 and Kamarudin*et al.*, 2014). As a result, analysing Revenue Efficiency also provides a partial view about the performance of banks as it takes into account the output side only. Practically, banks need to consider both input and output aspects to enhance the efficiency performance i.e. they have to focus on cost reduction as well as on revenue expansion simultaneously.

Thus, to get a comprehensive view of bank's performance, it is imperative to study Cost and Revenue Efficiency concepts simultaneously. Only a few studies in the literature available have evaluated Revenue Efficiency along with Cost Efficiency of the banks as Loukoianova (2008),Wanniarachchigeand Suzuki (2011),Pančurová and Lyócsa (2013) and García-Alcober*et al.* (2014).Loukoianova (2008)analyzed the Cost and Revenue Efficiency of Japanese banks from 2000 to 2006. The study reported that Japanese banks overall had Cost Efficiency of 69% and 70.8% according to Constant return to scale (CRS) and Variable Return to Scale (VRS) respectively. Average Revenue Efficiency of Japanese Banks was higher than Cost Efficiency as it stood at 93.3% and 87.8% according to Constant return to scale and Variable Return to Scale respectively. Wanniarachchigeand Suzuki (2011) estimated the performance of 50 Indian Commercial Banks in terms of Cost and Revenue Efficiency during 2002-2009 using Data Envelopment Analysis. The results showed that Revenue Efficiency decreased from 0.810 in 2001-02 to 0.586 in 2008-09 and Cost Efficiency decreased from 0.701 in 2001-02 to 0.673 in 2008-09. The results of efficiency across ownership depicted that Foreign Banks were most revenue efficient as well as cost efficient followed by State-Owned, Nationalized and Domestic Private Banks respectively. Pančurová and Lyócsa

(2013) estimated the Cost and Revenue Efficiency of 187 Commercial Banks operating in 11 Central and Eastern European Countries (CEEC) over 2005–2008 using Data Envelopment Analysis (DEA). The study observed that Cost Efficiency declined slightly from 33.6% in 2005 to 26.3% in 2008 while Revenue Efficiency increased from 42.1% in 2005 to 49.5% in 2008. The study found that all the countries had average Cost and Revenue Efficiency of 31.1% and 45.9% respectively from 2005-2008. García-Alcober *et al.* (2014) measured both Cost and Revenue Efficiency by applying Free Disposal Hull (FDH) and Data Envelopment Analysis (DEA). The results of the study showed that Commercial Banks were the most cost efficient banks while credit union banks had high Revenue Efficiency during pre-crisis and crisis time period. The robust tests results showed that efficiency scores had significant difference in pre crisis and post crisis period for all banks.

On exploring the literature covering Cost and Revenue Efficiency, it comes to light that only one study has been found for Indian banks that evaluated Cost and Revenue Efficiency simultaneously, namely, Wanniarachchige and Suzuki (2011). The study covers the time period till 2009, but it ignores the most critical time of recession aftermath wherein the economy took much time to stabilise itself and recoup its financial parameters. Also, the study limits itself to just 50 banks. The small sample size does not represent the whole banking sector and hence generalisation of results is difficult. In addition, efficiency is a relative measure of performance. Efficiency scores calculated on small sample may lead to biasness in results. Moreover, the study fails to identify the reasons behind cost and revenue inefficiency. Hence, there is a need to plug the gap and reassess all SCBs operating in India with respect to the Cost and Revenue Efficiency scores especially in the current dynamic environment. Dynamism leads to uncertainty and risk (Liem and Hien, 2019). Banking Sector has been witnessing the same since long; first due to LPG reforms then the macro-economic upheavals like recession, followed by electronic upgradation phenomenon etc. Thus, the present paper uses unbalanced panel data of the Indian Scheduled Commercial Banks existing and employs a non parametric approach namely, Data Envelopment Analysis (DEA) to estimate Cost Efficiency and Revenue Efficiency over the period 2002-03 to 2012-13.

The paper proceeds as follows. Section 1 introduces the topic of the study and reviews the available literature. Section 2 presents the objectives of the study. Section 3 explains the database and methodology used. Section 4 describes the various inputs-outputs and their prices used to measure the efficiency of the banks. Section 5 presents the results. Finally, Section 6 draws conclusions and outlines some suggestions for future work.

Objectives of the Study

The primary objective of the study is to analyze and evaluate Cost and Revenue Efficiency scores of Scheduled Commercial Banks (SCBs) operating in India. In addition, cost and Revenue Efficiency is analyzed across bank ownership as well. The paper also determines reasons behind the cost and revenue inefficiency among Scheduled Commercial Banks (SCBs) operating in India.

Database and Methodology

Database

The sample of the study includes all commercial banks operating in India during 2000-01 to 2016-17. The number of observations varies across time due to missing observations for some banks for certain years. The effective sample of the study is given in a tabular format as follows in Table: 1

Table: 1 Sample of the Study

YEAR	Public Sector Banks	Private Sector Banks	Foreign Sector Banks	Indian Scheduled Commercial Bank
2000-01	27	31	37	95
2004-05	28	29	26	83
2008-09	27	20	21	68
2012-13	26	20	30	76
2016-17	27	21	43	91

The study covers the time period of 2000-01 to 2016-17. It is split over five points of time i.e. 2000-01, 2004-05, 2008-09, 2012-13 and 2016-17 to assess the efficiency scores intermittently after a uniform gap of three years each in order to bring consistency and robustness in analyses. 2000-01 is beginning of electronic decade for banks after exhaustion of ten years from the reformatory phase. Since 2004-05, major changes in banking sector took place as Indian Financial Network (INFINET) was introduced which enabled faster connectivity within the financial sector. Further, e-banking, Basel Norms, Know Your Customer (KYC), Debt Recovery Tribunals and Anti-money Laundering (AML) etc were introduced during this phase. However, 2008-09 was depressing for the banks due to spill over effects of global financial recession. 2012-13 is assumed to be the post crisis period where the economy is perceived to have recovered it and 2016-17 marks the most recent time period. The present study gathers data from website of Reserve Bank of India (RBI) which is considered as the most reliable database for research in banking.

Data Envelopment Analysis (DEA)

DEA is a linear programming based technique employed for assessing the relative performance of a set of firms against the best-observed performance. It constructs the frontier of the most efficient firms of the sample and then measures how far the other firms are from the frontiers. A firm in DEA is known as Decision Making Unit (DMU). DEA assigns each DMU a single efficiency score that allows ranking amongst DMUs in the sample (Sufian, 2009). The firm having score of one is the most efficient firm, while the firm having score between zero and one is less efficient. DEA also permits to diagnose the causes of inefficiencies in order to identify the areas for improvement i.e. whether the input has been excessively used or the output has been produced less. In the present paper, DEA is used to compute Cost Efficiency (CE) and Revenue Efficiency (RE) of banks.

A Cost Efficiency model is an input oriented model, as it minimizes inputs at a given level of output quantities and input prices. To identify the reasons of cost inefficiency among banks, Cost Efficiency can further be decomposed into Allocative Efficiency (AE) (input oriented) and Technical Efficiency (TE) (input oriented) components. In other words,

Cost Efficiency = Technical Efficiency (Input Oriented) × Allocative Efficiency (Input Oriented)

Allocative Efficiency (AE) (input oriented) evaluates the capability of the bank to utilize minimum inputs to generate the given outputs as well as considering the input prices. Technical Efficiency (TE) (input oriented) is the ability of the firm to minimize their input to produce the given set of outputs.

A Revenue Efficiency model is an output oriented model that maximizes revenue for a given set of input quantities and output prices. Furthermore, to detect the reasons of revenue inefficiency, Revenue Efficiency is decomposed in to technical and allocative efficiency (output oriented). It can be written as:

Revenue Efficiency = Technical Efficiency (Output Oriented) × Allocative Efficiency (Output Oriented)

Allocative Efficiency (AE) (output oriented) evaluates the capability of the bank in producing revenue maximizing mix of outputs based on output prices (Kamarudin *et al.*, 2014). It refers to the ability to combine inputs and outputs in optimal proportion in the light of prevailing prices (Lovell, 1993). Technical Efficiency (TE) (output oriented) is the ability of the firm to maximize output from the given set of inputs. It refers to the ability to avoid waste by giving as much output as input usage permits (Lovell, 1993). The following is the mathematical programming equation used to calculate Cost and Revenue Efficiency present in Table: 2:

Table: 2 Mathematical Formulation of Efficiency

Cost Efficiency	Revenue Efficiency
$\text{Min} = \sum_{r=1}^{m} p_i^o \tilde{x}_{io}$ Subject to $\sum_{j=1}^{n} \lambda_j x_{ij} \leq \tilde{x}_{io}$ $i = 1, 2, \ldots, m$ $\sum_{i=1}^{n} \lambda_j y_{rj} \geq y_{ro}$ $r = 1, 2, \ldots, s$ $\lambda_j, \tilde{x}_{io} \geq 0$ $\sum_{i=1}^{n} \lambda_j = 1$	$\text{Max} = \sum_{r=1}^{s} q_r^o \tilde{y}_{ro}$ Subject to $\sum_{j=1}^{n} \lambda_j x_{ij} \leq \tilde{x}_{io}$ $i = 1, 2, \ldots, m$ $\sum_{i=1}^{n} \lambda_j y_{rj} \geq \tilde{y}_{ro}$ $r = 1, 2, \ldots, s$ $\lambda_j, \tilde{y}_{ro} \geq 0$ $\sum_{i=1}^{n} \lambda_j = 1$

Source: Zhu (2009)

where,

n = DMU observation

j = n^{th} DMU

s = output observation

m = input observation

r = s^{th} output

i = m^{th} input

q_r^o = unit price of the output r of DMU_0

y_{ro} = r^{th} output that maximise revenue for DMU0

$\tilde{x}_{io}$ = i^{th} input that minimise cost for DMU0

y_{ro} = r^{th} output for DMU0

x_{io} = i^{th} input for DMU0

y_{rj} = s^{th} output for nth DMU

x_{ij} = m^{th} input for nth DMU

λj = non-negative scalars

DEA can further help to decompose Technical Efficiency (both input and output oriented) into its components, Pure Technical Efficiency and Scale Efficiency (Coelli, 1998; Sufian, 2004). This decomposition helps to detect the reasons of technical inefficiencies which can be due to the inefficient implementation of the production plan in converting inputs to outputs (pure technical inefficiency) or due to divergence of a bank from the most productive scale size (scale inefficiency). In other words,

Technical Efficiency = Pure Technical Efficiency × Scale Efficiency

Selection of Banking Inputs and Outputs

For calculating the efficiency scores of banks, selection of inputs and outputs is an important but a controversial issue in banking (Ariff and Can, 2008 and Berger and Humphrey, 1997). The results of efficiency scores may vary depending on the selection of variables for each of the banks' efficiency (Forughi and De Zoysa, 2012 and Kamarudin *et al.*, 2014). The study based on efficiency of banks widely follows either Operating Approach or Intermediation Approach. The operating approach considers banks as using purchased inputs to produce deposits and various categories of bank assets whereas intermediation approach considers banks as intermediaries that use deposits together with other inputs such as labor and capital to produce the outputs like loans and advances. Intermediation approach is mostly preferred among researchers to evaluate the efficiency of the banks for the reason that intermediate approach suits more to the nature of the banking industry than production approach (Benston, 1965 and Berger and Humphrey, 1997). Following the intermediation approach, this article uses four inputs and two outputs. In order to calculate the Cost and Revenue Efficiency input and output prices are required. The description of inputs, outputs and their prices are presented in Table: 3.

Table: 3 Description of Input and Output Variables.

Variables	Description
Input Variables	
• Deposits	Demand Deposits + Term Deposit + Savings Deposits.
• Borrowings	Borrowings from RBI and other Banks or Financial institutions.
• Fixed Assets	Premises + Fixed Assets under Construction + Other fixed Assets.
• Number of Employees	Number of Employees working in the banks.
Output Variables	
• Investments	Investments in Approved Securities, Government Securities, other approved securities, shares, debentures.
• Loans and Advances	Term Loans + Cash Credit, Overdraft + Bills purchased and discounted etc.
• Non-Interest income	Commission + Bill Discounted + Fee.
Input Prices	
• Price of Deposits	Interest paid on Deposits/Deposits.
• Price of Borrowings	Interest paid on borrowings from RBI and other agencies/Borrowing.
• Price of Fixed Assets	(Rent, Taxes and Lighting + Depreciation on Banks' assets + Repair and Maintenance + Insurance)/Fixed Assets.
• Price of number of employees	Payment and provisions for employees/ number of employees.
Output Prices	
• Prices of Investments	Income (interest and dividend received) from Investments/Investments.
• Prices of Loan and Advances	Interest received from loans and advances/ Loans and Advances.
• Prices of Non-Interest Income	Price of non-interest income as unity throughout the years for all banks.

Findings and Discussion

Assessment of Cost Efficiency and Revenue Efficiency of Scheduled Commercial Banks in India

Table: 4 depicts year wise average Cost Efficiency, Revenue Efficiency and its components scores of all Scheduled Commercial Banks operating in India over five points of time as 2000-01, 2004-05, 2008-09, 2012-13 and 2016-17.

Table: 4 Cost Efficiency and Revenue Efficiency Scores of Indian Scheduled Commercial Banks

YEAR	No. of Banks	CE	AE (IO)	TE (IO)	PTE (IO)	SE (IO)	RE	AE (OO)	TE (OO)	PTE (OO)	SE (OO)
2000-01	95	0.548	0.643	0.854	0.943	0.905	0.690	0.807	0.854	0.946	0.902
2004-05	83	0.685	0.747	0.914	0.971	0.941	0.658	0.714	0.914	0.968	0.944
2008-09	68	0.713	0.795	0.896	0.978	0.915	0.722	0.804	0.896	0.979	0.914
2012-13	76	0.493	0.567	0.870	0.966	0.898	0.572	0.658	0.870	0.965	0.900
2016-17	91	0.514	0.694	0.742	0.976	0.761	0.529	0.714	0.742	0.977	0.759

Cost Efficiency of Scheduled Commercial Banks in India

Cost Efficiency (inefficiency) of Scheduled Commercial Banks operating in India is 54.8% (45.2%) in 2000-01. This depicts that on an average Scheduled Commercial Banks operating in India exploit only 54.8% of their inputs to produce the current output. Average allocative efficiency (input oriented) (inefficiency) is 64.3% (35.7%) whereas Technical Efficiency (input oriented) (in efficiency) is 85.4% (14.6%). Pure technical and Scale Efficiency (input oriented) (inefficiency) of Scheduled Commercial Banks is 94.3% (5.7%) and 90.5% (9.5%) respectively. In 2004-05, Scheduled Commercial Banks operating in India could utilize only 68.5% of the inputs to produce the same level of outputs and they wasted 31.5% of its inputs. Allocative efficiency (input oriented) is 74.7% whereas Technical Efficiency (input oriented) is 91.4%. Further, pure technical (input oriented) and Scale Efficiency (input oriented) of Scheduled Commercial Banks is 97.1% and 94.1% respectively for the year 2004-05.

The Cost Efficiency (inefficiency) of Scheduled Commercial Banks operating in India is 71.3% (28.7%) in 2008-09. The average Allocative efficiency, Technical Efficiency, Pure Technical Efficiency and Scale Efficiency (input oriented) is 79.5%, 89.6%, 97.8% and 91.5%, respectively. Scheduled Commercial Banks on an average could use only 49.3% of resources in 2012-13 while they wasted the remaining resources. In 2012-13, average Allocative efficiency (input oriented) is 56.7% whereas Technical Efficiency (input oriented) is 87.0%. Further, Pure Technical (input oriented) and Scale Efficiency (input oriented) of Scheduled Commercial Banks is 96.6% and 89.8% respectively for the year 2012-13. Scheduled Commercial Banks operating in India could utilize only 51.4% of the inputs to produce the same level of outputs and they wasted 48.6% of its inputs in 2016-17. Allocative efficiency (input oriented) is 69.4% whereas Technical Efficiency (input oriented) is 74.2%. Further, pure technical (input oriented) and Scale Efficiency (input oriented) of Scheduled Commercial Banks is 97.6% and 76.1% respectively in the year 2016-17.

The Efficiency in 2000-01 is somewhat low this might be due to the reason that importance was given to computerization in the beginning of 2000s. The massive cost incurred on infrastructure and technological up-gradations which escorted banks to low Cost Efficiency. A hike in Cost Efficiency scores is witnessed in 2004-05 due to reduced the wage bill on account of Voluntary Retirement Schemes (VRS) introduced in 2000-01. Indian Scheduled Commercial Banks made a noticeable shift in switching from paper-based transactions to electronic means as Real Time Gross Settlement (RTGS), National Electronic Fund

Transfer (NEFT) and other electronic modes helped them to reduce their transaction cost and expand their outreach especially in the remote and rural areas raising the Cost Efficiency to 71.3% by the end of 2008-09. A deep decline in the Cost Efficiency of SCBs during 2012-13 seems to be on account of moderate global recovery from the ripples of global financial recession. This is perhaps due to the reason that SCBs' low-cost current and saving account (CASA) deposits posted marginally higher growth as compared to the previous year.

Cost Efficiency is the multiplicative combination of Allocative Efficiency and Technical Efficiency (input oriented). As seen from Table: 4, Technical Efficiency scores (input oriented) have always been higher than Allocative Efficiency scores. Thus the dominant reason behind Cost Inefficiency is Allocative Inefficiency. Higher Allocative Inefficiency (input oriented) demonstrates that bank managers are quite incapable of selecting the cost minimizing mix of inputs at the given input prices. On the other hand, Technical Efficiency (input oriented) scores are still less than 1 which is the standard efficiency score. Thus the detection of Technical Inefficiency reveals that Scale inefficiency is constantly higher than Pure Technical Inefficiency among SCBs. Thus SCBs need to think about their input usage to improve upon their Cost Efficiency.

Revenue Efficiency of Scheduled Commercial Banks in India

Revenue Efficiency (inefficiency) of Scheduled Commercial Banks operating in India is 69.0% (31.0%) in 2000-01. This depicts that on an average Scheduled Commercial Banks operating in India could generate only 69.0% revenue from their available inputs. Average allocative efficiency (output oriented) (inefficiency) is 80.7% (19.3%) whereas Technical Efficiency(output oriented) (inefficiency) is 85.4% (14.6%). Pure technical and Scale Efficiency (output oriented) (inefficiency) of Scheduled Commercial Banks is 94.6% (5.4%) and 90.2% (9.8%) respectively. In 2004-05, Scheduled Commercial Banks operating in India could generate only 65.8% of revenue which is less than what they were expected to generate from the same inputs. Allocative efficiency (output oriented) is 71.4% whereas Technical Efficiency (output oriented)is 91.4%. Further, pure technical and Scale Efficiency(output oriented) of Scheduled Commercial Banksis 96.8% and 94.4% respectively for the year 2004-05.

The Revenue Efficiency (output oriented) (inefficiency) of Scheduled Commercial Banks operating in India is 72.2% (27.8%) in 2008-09. The average allocative efficiency, Technical Efficiency, Pure Technical Efficiency and Scale Efficiency(output oriented) is 80.4%, 89.6%, 97.9% and 91.4%, respectively. Scheduled Commercial Banks on an average could generate only 57.2% of revenue in 2012-13 which is again less than what they were expected to generate from the same inputs. In 2012-13, average allocative efficiency(output oriented) is 65.8% whereas Technical Efficiency (output oriented) is 87.0%. Further, Pure technical and Scale Efficiency(output oriented) of Scheduled Commercial Banks is 96.5% and 90.0%, respectively, for the year 2012-13. The Revenue Efficiency (output oriented) (inefficiency) of Scheduled Commercial Banks operating in India is 52.9% (47.1%) in 2016-17. The average allocative efficiency, Technical Efficiency, Pure Technical Efficiency and Scale Efficiency (output oriented) is 71.4%, 74.2%, 97.7% and 75.9%, respectively.

Revenue Efficiency of Indian Scheduled Commercial Banks in 2000-01 is not very high. Interest has been primary source of bank income, followed by non-interest income. The year 2000-01 witnessed deceleration both in the interest income and the non-interest income of banks. The ratio of interest income to total assets lowered to 6.7% in 2004-05 from 8.88% in 2000-01 and non-interest income to total assets fell to 1.5% from 1.32% in 2000-01 hampering the Revenue Efficiency of the banks further in 2004-05 (Reserve Bank of India, 2004-05). The asset quality of banks' improved in 2008-09 due to hard efforts put in by authorities. The same is reflected by declining ratio of gross NPAs to gross advances from 5.2% in 2004-05 to 2.3% in 2008-09 (Reserve Bank of India, 2008-09). This is attributable to the cascading effect of decline in the growth of profits of Scheduled Commercial Banks (SCBs) due to the slowing down of credit off-take and lesser interest rates. A downfall in the Revenue Efficiency is noticed in 2012-13 and 2016-17. SCBs' interest earnings and non-interest incomes were adversely affected (Reserve Bank of India, 2016-17) which evidently showed its impact on Revenue Efficiency score.

The methodological framework of DEA highlights that Technical Efficiency and allocative efficiency (output oriented) constitute Revenue Efficiency. As a result, to determine the causes of revenue inefficiency, technical and allocative efficiency are required to be analyzed. Table:4 indicates that allocative inefficiency has always been smaller than technical inefficiency. Thus the dominant source of revenue inefficiency is technical inefficiency. The higher technical inefficiency comparative with allocative inefficiency implies that managers are relatively good at choosing the revenue maximizing mix of outputat given output prices, but they are not good at producing maximum output from a given input. Furthermore, the decomposition of Technical Efficiency (output oriented) into its components could help in detecting the sources of technical inefficiency. Table: 4 shows Pure Technical Efficiency scores higher than Scale Efficiency scores for all the years under study. This suggests that the greater part of inefficiency among Scheduled Commercial Banks operating in India is attributed to scale inefficiency. Scale inefficiency cautions that banks are not operating on the optimum scale. They need to expand their business not only by opening new branches, but also by increasing their customer base by indulging in quality services and effective customer relation management to achieve economies of scale.

Analysis of Cost Efficiency vis-à-vis Revenue Efficiency of Scheduled Commercial Banks in India

As depicted from the results of Cost Efficiency and Revenue Efficiency, the highest level of inefficiency subsisted on the cost side as Scheduled Commercial Banks have higher Revenue Efficiency score in comparison to Cost Efficiency scores. SCBs had adopted modernisation and offered electronic banking, Mobile Banking, Credit Card, Automatic Teller Machines (ATM), Electronic Fund Transfers (EFTs), Real Time Gross settlement (RTGs) and National Electronic Fund Transfer (NEFTs) etc. These advancements increased their cost resulting into temporary cost inefficiency. But it is worth mentioning that these investments in technological advancements enhanced the revenues of banks by enabling them to provide quality services and helping them sustain their market share against Non-banking Financial Institutions and other financial houses. Also, Scheduled Commercial Banks (SCBs) exhibited greater emphasis on product diversification and adoption of information technology for providing quality services to customers which helped them to enhance their revenues. SCBs also framed customer orientated strategies in order to meet thrust towards retail banking and thus enhance the revenues.

Assessment of Cost Efficiency and Revenue Efficiency of Scheduled Commercial Banks in India Across Ownership

The Indian Banking is predominantly attractive because of the diversity of bank ownership structure. Indian banks are divided into three groups, i.e. Public, Private and Foreign Sector Banks. These groups of banks have a different set of regulations but they all function in the same market. It is imperative to recognize as to which particular sector is leading to anxious results in the overall efficiency scores. Hence, we now conduct an efficiency evaluation of SCBs across ownership. The sector wise average efficiency scores are presented as follows in Table: 5:

Table: 5 Cost Efficiency and Revenue Efficiency Scores of Indian Scheduled Commercial Banks across Ownership

	Public Sector Banks					Private Sector Banks					Foreign Sector Banks				
Cost Efficiency															
YEAR	CE	AE (IO)	TE (IO)	PTE (IO)	SE (IO)	CE	AE (IO)	TE (IO)	PTE (IO)	SE (IO)	CE	AE (IO)	TE (IO)	PTE (IO)	SE (IO)
2000-01	0.578	0.641	0.896	0.976	0.919	0.496	0.595	0.837	0.922	0.909	0.569	0.685	0.839	0.937	0.891
2004-05	0.684	0.738	0.926	0.986	0.940	0.702	0.766	0.907	0.956	0.950	0.668	0.735	0.908	0.971	0.932
2008-09	0.650	0.755	0.866	0.983	0.880	0.698	0.803	0.869	0.953	0.911	0.808	0.838	0.960	0.996	0.964
2012-13	0.368	0.419	0.884	0.980	0.902	0.431	0.544	0.807	0.952	0.847	0.642	0.711	0.899	0.964	0.929
2016-17	0.401	0.707	0.568	0.980	0.578	0.397	0.664	0.597	0.972	0.613	0.634	0.691	0.922	0.976	0.944
Revenue Efficiency															
YEAR	RE	AE (OO)	TE (OO)	PTE (OO)	SE (OO)	RE	AE (OO)	TE (OO)	PTE (OO)	SE (OO)	RE	AE (OO)	TE (OO)	PTE (OO)	SE (OO)
2000-01	0.749	0.831	0.896	0.978	0.917	0.625	0.751	0.837	0.925	0.906	0.702	0.837	0.839	0.940	0.889
2004-05	0.732	0.786	0.926	0.987	0.939	0.626	0.683	0.907	0.957	0.948	0.615	0.672	0.908	0.962	0.943
2008-09	0.681	0.785	0.866	0.984	0.880	0.743	0.850	0.869	0.955	0.909	0.754	0.785	0.960	0.997	0.964
2012-13	0.518	0.587	0.884	0.980	0.901	0.624	0.767	0.807	0.953	0.846	0.585	0.647	0.899	0.961	0.935
2016-17	0.552	0.973	0.567	0.981	0.577	0.408	0.685	0.597	0.974	0.612	0.685	0.743	0.922	0.978	0.942

CE: Cost Efficiency, AE (IO): Allocative Efficiency (Input Oriented), TE (IO): Technical Efficiency (Input Oriented), PTE (IO): Pure Technical Efficiency (Input Oriented), SE (IO): Scale Efficiency(Input Oriented), RE: Revenue Efficiency, AE (OO): Allocative Efficiency (Output Oriented), TE (OO): Technical Efficiency (Output Oriented), PTE (OO): Pure Technical Efficiency (Output Oriented), SE (OO): Scale Efficiency (Output Oriented)

Cost Efficiency of Public Sector Banks in India

Table: 5 presents the Revenue and Cost Efficiency scores over five points of time for Public, Private and Foreign Sector Banks. It is observed that in 2000-01, Cost Efficiency (inefficiency) of Public Sector Banks operating in India is 57.8% (42.2%). Average allocative efficiency (input oriented) is 64.1% (35.9%) whereas Technical Efficiency is 89.6% (10.4%). Pure technical and Scale Efficiency of Public Sector Banks is 97.6% (2.4%) and 91.9% (8.1%) respectively. Public Sector Banks operating in India could utilize only 68.4% of resources in 2004-05 to produce what they are producing today and wasting 31.6% of resources. In 2004-05, average allocative efficiency is 73.8% (26.2%) whereas Technical Efficiency is 92.6% (7.4%). Further, pure technical and Scale Efficiency of Public Sector Banks is 98.6% (1.4%) and 94.0% (6.0%), respectively for the year 2004-05. In 2008-09, Cost Efficiency of Public Sector Banks operating in India is 65.0% (35.0%). Average allocative efficiency, Technical Efficiency, Pure Technical Efficiency and Scale Efficiency is 75.5%, 86.6%, 98.3% and 88.0%, respectively. Public Sector Banks use only 36.8% of inputs actually employed in 2012-13, to produce the same level of output in this year. In other words, the average input waste was 63.2% of inputs. In 2012-13, average allocative efficiency is 41.9% whereas Technical Efficiency is 88.4%. Further, pure technical and Scale Efficiency of Public Sector Banks is 98.0% (2%) and 90.2% (9.8%) respectively for the year 2012-13. Public Sector Banks operating in India could utilize only 40.1% of resources in 2016-17 to produce what they are producing from their resources. In 2016-17, average allocative efficiency is 70.7% whereas Technical Efficiency is 56.8%. Further, pure technical and Scale Efficiency of Public Sector Banks is 98.0% and 57.8% respectively for the year 2016-17.

Cost Efficiency of Private Sector Banks in India

Private Sector Banks (on an average) could utilize only 49.6% of resources in 2000-01 thus wasting the rest of resources. In 2000-01, average allocative efficiency is 59.5% (40.5%) whereas Technical Efficiency is 83.7% (16.3%). Further, pure technical and Scale Efficiency of Private Sector Banks is 92.2% (7.8%) and 90.9% (9.1%), respectively, for the year 2000-01. Cost Efficiency of Private Sector Banks operating in India is 70.2% (29.8%) in 2004-05. Average allocative efficiency, Technical Efficiency, Pure Technical Efficiency and Scale Efficiency is 76.6%, 90.7%, 95.6% and 95.0%, respectively. Cost Efficiency (inefficiency) of Private Sector Banks operating in India is 69.8% (30.2%) in 2008-09. Average allocative efficiency is 80.3% whereas Technical Efficiency is 86.9%. Pure technical and Scale Efficiency of Private Sector Banks is 95.3% and 91.1% respectively. Private Sector Banks (on an average) could utilize only 43.1% of resources in 2012-13. Average allocative efficiency is 54.4% (45.6%) whereas Technical Efficiency is 80.7% (19.3%). Further, pure technical and Scale Efficiency of Private Sector Banks is 95.2% (4.8%) and 84.7% (15.3%), respectively, for the year 2012-13. Private Sector Banks (on an average) could utilize only 39.7% of resources in 2016-17 thus wasting the rest of resources. In 2016-17, average allocative efficiency is 66.4% whereas Technical Efficiency is 59.7%. Further, pure technical and Scale Efficiency of Private Sector Banks is 97.2% and 61.3% respectively, for the year 2016-17.

Cost Efficiency of Foreign Sector Banks in India

Cost Efficiency (inefficiency) of Foreign Sector Banks operating in India is 56.9% (43.1%) in 2000-01. Average Allocative efficiency is 68.5% (31.5%) whereas Technical Efficiency is 83.9% (16.1%). Pure technical and Scale Efficiency of Foreign Sector Banks is 93.7% (6.3%) and 89.1% (10.9%), respectively. In the year 2004-05, Cost Efficiency (inefficiency) of Foreign Sector Banks operating in India is 66.8% (18.8%). Average Allocative efficiency, Technical Efficiency, Pure Technical Efficiency and Scale Efficiency is 73.5%, 90.8%, 97.1% and 93.2%, respectively, in 2004-05. Foreign Sector Banks operating

in India could utilize only 80.8% of inputs in 2008-09. In 2008-09, average allocative efficiency (inefficiency) is 83.8% (16.2%) whereas Technical Efficiency is 96.0% (4.0%). Further, pure technical and Scale Efficiency of Foreign Sector Banks is 99.6% and 96.4%, respectively, for the year 2008-09. Foreign Sector Banks on an average could exploit only 64.2% of resources in 2012-13 to produce what they are producing while wasting 35.8% of resources. In 2012-13, average Allocative efficiency is 71.1% (28.9%) whereas Technical Efficiency is 89.9% (10.1%). Further, pure technical and Scale Efficiency (inefficiency) of Foreign Sector Banks is 96.4% (3.6%) and 92.9% (7.1%) respectively for the year 2012-13. In the year 2016-17, Cost Efficiency (inefficiency) of Foreign Sector Banks operating in India is 63.4%. Average Allocative efficiency, Technical Efficiency, Pure Technical Efficiency and Scale Efficiency is 69.1%, 92.2%, 97.1% and 94.4%, respectively, in 2016-17.

Analysis of Cost Efficiency (Inefficiency) in Public vis-à-vis Private vis-à-vis Foreign Sector Banks

Public Sector Banks have been facing the problem of surplus manpower resources since long depicted by wage bill to total assets provides an evidence of this inefficiency. In order to reduce this cost, PSBs offered Voluntary Retirement Scheme (VRS) to the employees in 2000-01 which gradually decreased their operating cost depicting better Cost Efficiency. A rise in interest expenditure to 5.14% in 2008-09 (Reserve Bank of India, 2008-09) and further to 5.57% in 2012-13 (Reserve Bank of India, 2012-13) deteriorated the Cost Efficiency scores. A high and rising proportion of banks' delinquent loans in case of public sector banks (PSBs) increased the provisioning for non-performing assets which resulted in stressed financial position of Public sector Banks. Private Sector Banks had made huge investment in upgrading their technology at the inception of electronic era in 2000s. Such massive capital expenditure at a point of time led to anxious Cost Efficiency scores. Private Sector Banks lowered their interest expenditure which led to improvement in the Cost Efficiency. A hike in interest expenditure seemed to have escorted banks to poor Cost Efficiency score.

The same is evident from the ratio of interest expenditure to total assets which increased from 3.80% in 2004-05 to 5.54% in 2008-09. The cost of deposits increased from 6.43% in 2011-12 to 6.72% in 2012-13 (Reserve Bank of India, 2012-13). This brought Cost Efficiency score of Private Sector Banks to a low level. Private sector banks witnessed higher growth in Current and saving account deposits which increased their cost of deposits hence leads to lower cost efficiency. Foreign Sector Banks too have been paying high rate of interest to attract customers. In 2004-05 the interest expenditure witnessed decrease owing to the reason that Benchmark Prime Lending Rates (BPLRs) (Reserve Bank of India, 2004-05). The ratio of operating expenditure to total assets decreased from 2.87% in 2004-05 to 2.76% in 2008-09. This tends to increase the Cost Efficiency of Foreign Sector Banks. In order to retain and sustain customers after US recession, Foreign Sector Banks had also offered high rate of interest on deposits. Foreign Sector Banks witnessed higher growth in Current and saving account deposits which increased their cost of deposits hence leads to lower cost efficiency.

As seen from Table: 5, Technical Efficiency (Input Oriented) scores of all banks operating in different sectors are better than Allocative Efficiency scores in all the years of the study. Thus the foremost reason behind cost inefficiency of Public Sector Banks, Private Sector Banks and Foreign Sector Banks is allocative inefficiency. Further, the main source of technical inefficiency (input oriented) is attributed to scale inefficiency among Public Sector Banks, Private Sector Banks and Foreign Sector Banks. Thus, the results highlight that banks operating in different sectors are not operating on the most advantageous scale. It can be concluded that all banks are facing the problem of attaining the desired scale i.e. either they are operating on Increasing or Decreasing Return to Scale. Scale inefficiency seems to be a major cause of poor performance of banks operating in different sectors in India. This implies that majority of banks need to enlarge their scale of operations.

Revenue Efficiency of Public Sector Banks in India

Table: 5 also highlights the Revenue Efficiency scores of banks in different sectors. Revenue Efficiency (inefficiency) of Public Sector Banks operating in India is 74.9% (25.1%) in 2000-01. Average Allocative efficiency is 83.1% (16.9%) whereas Technical Efficiency is 89.6% (10.4%). Pure technical and Scale Efficiency of Public Sector Banks is 97.8% (2.2%) and 91.7% (8.3%) respectively. Public Sector Banks operating in India could generate only 73.2% of revenue in 2004-05, which is less than what they were expected to generate from the same inputs. In 2004-05, average allocative efficiency is 78.6% (21.4%) whereas Technical Efficiency is 92.6% (7.4%). Further, pure technical and Scale Efficiency of Public Sector Banks is 98.7% (1.3%) and 93.9% (6.1%), respectively, for the year 2004-05. Revenue Efficiency of Public Sector Banks operating in India is 68.1% (31.9%) in 2008-09. Average allocative efficiency, Technical Efficiency, Pure Technical Efficiency and Scale Efficiency is 78.5%, 86.6%, 98.4% and 88.0%, respectively. Public Sector Banks on average could generate only 51.8% of revenue in 2012-13, which is less than what they were expected to generate from the same inputs. In 2012-13, average allocative efficiency is 58.7% whereas Technical Efficiency is 88.4%. Further, pure technical and Scale Efficiency of Public Sector Banks is 98.0% (2%) and 90.1% (9.9%) respectively for the year 2012-13. Revenue Efficiency of Public Sector Banks operating in India is 55.2% in 2016-17. Average allocative efficiency, Technical Efficiency, Pure Technical Efficiency and Scale Efficiency is 97.3%, 56.7%, 98.1% and 57.7%, respectively.

Revenue Efficiency of Private Sector Banks in India

Private Sector Banks on an average could generate only 62.5% of revenue in 2000-01, less than what they were expected to generate from the same inputs. In 2000-01, average Allocative efficiency is 75.1% (24.9%) whereas Technical Efficiency is 83.7% (16.3%). Further, Pure Technical and Scale Efficiency of Private Sector Banks is 92.5% (7.5%) and 90.6% (9.4%) respectively for the year 2000-01. The Revenue Efficiency of Private Sector Banks operating in India is 62.6% (37.4%) in 2004-05. Average Allocative efficiency, Technical Efficiency, Pure Technical Efficiency and Scale Efficiency is 68.3%, 90.7%, 95.7% and 94.8% respectively. The Revenue Efficiency (inefficiency) of Private Sector Banks operating in India is 74.3% (25.7%) in 2008-09. Average Allocative efficiency is 85.0% whereas Technical Efficiency is 86.9%. Pure Technical and Scale Efficiency of Private Sector Banks is 95.5% and 90.9% respectively. Private Sector Banks operating in India could generate only 62.4% of revenue in 2012-13, which is less than what they were expected to generate from the same inputs. In 2012-13, average Allocative efficiency is 76.7% (23.3%) whereas Technical Efficiency is 80.7% (19.3%). Further, Pure Technical and Scale Efficiency of Private Sector Banks is 95.3% (6.5%) and 84.6% (15.4%) respectively for the year 2012-13. Revenue Efficiency of Private Sector Banks operating in India is 40.8% in 2016-17. Average allocative efficiency, Technical Efficiency, Pure Technical Efficiency and Scale Efficiency is 68.5%, 59.7%, 97.4% and 61.2%, respectively.

Revenue Efficiency of Foreign Sector Banks in India

Revenue Efficiency (inefficiency) of Foreign Sector Banks operating in India is 70.2% (29.8%) in 2000-01. Average allocative efficiency is 83.7% (16.3%) whereas Technical Efficiency is 83.9% (16.1%). Pure technical and Scale Efficiency of Foreign Sector Banks is 94.0% (6.0%) and 88.9% (11.1%), respectively. In the year 2004-05, Revenue Efficiency (inefficiency) of Foreign Sector Banks operating in India is 61.5% (38.5%). Average allocative efficiency, Technical Efficiency, Pure Technical Efficiency and Scale Efficiency is 67.2%, 90.8%, 96.2% and 94.3%, respectively in 2004-05. Foreign Sector Banks operating in India could generate only 75.4% of revenue in 2008-09, which is less than what they were expected to generate from the same inputs. In 2008-09, average allocative efficiency (inefficiency) is 78.5% (21.5%) whereas Technical Efficiency is 96.0% (4.0%). Further, pure technical and Scale Efficiency of Foreign Sector Banks is 99.7% and 96.4%, respectively for the year 2008-09. Foreign Sector Banks on an average could generate only 58.5% of revenue in 2012-13, less than what they had anticipated to generate from the same inputs. In 2012-13, average allocative efficiency is 64.7% (35.3%) whereas Technical Efficiency is 89.9% (10.1%). Further, pure technical and Scale Efficiency (inefficiency) of Foreign Sector Banks is 96.1% (3.9%) and 93.5% (6.5%) respectively for the year 2012-13. Revenue Efficiency of Foreign Sector Banks operating in India is 68.5% in 2016-17. Average allocative efficiency, Technical Efficiency, Pure Technical Efficiency and Scale Efficiency is 74.3%, 92.2%, 97.8% and 94.2%, respectively.

Analysis of Revenue Efficiency (Inefficiency) in Public vis-à-vis Private vis-à-vis Foreign Sector Banks

In order to counter intense competition in the market, PSBs were forced to provide banking services at minimum returns. As a result the interest income to total assets of Public Sector Banks reduced from 18.88% in 1999-2000 to 18.46% in 2000-01. The trend continued till 2004-05 with the ratio lowering to 12.66%. In the successive years also market uncertainties resulting from global crisis did not let PSBs heave a sigh of relief, further lowering the Revenue Efficiency scores in 2008-09. The poor asset quality of PSBs added fuel to the fire. The rise in NPAs from 1.97% in 2008-09 till 2.02% in 2012-13 (Reserve Banks of India, 2013) further marred the Revenue Efficiency of PSBs. Private Sector Banks developed their customer base manifold by providing customers with innovative and prompt services (Jain, 2011). They had even started offering fee based services like merchant banking, cash management services, credit rating services, online trading facilities to the Demat account holders, tie up with the Government companies for opening salary accounts of the employees etc along with accepting deposits and lending funds. This seems to have accelerated their Revenue Efficiency scores from 0.625 in 2000-01, to 0.626 in 2004-05 and further to 0.743 in 2008-09. However, decreased relative Revenue Efficiency scores of Private Sector Banks in 2012-13 show their inability to generate maximum revenues from the available inputs given their output prices. Foreign Sector Banks (FSBs) lend loans and advances to them at lower interest rates as compared to their domestic counterparts. This affects their revenues. The same is evident from the ratio of interest income to total assets ratio which reduced from 7.68% in 2002-03, to 5.95% in 2004-05 (Reserve Bank of India, 2003-04). Thus, the Revenue Efficiency scores of Foreign Sector Banks diminished in 2004-05 as against 2000-01. The year 2008-09 witnessed augmentation in both the interest income as well as non-interest income of Foreign Sector Banks. This augmentation highlights their good performance thus enhancing their Revenue Efficiency scores. A significant observation also suggests that Revenue Efficiency of Foreign Sector Banks declined to their lowest in 2012-13. After the global financial crisis, Foreign Sector Banks had reduced their long term lending and shifted to short term exposures as far as granting of loans was concerned. Interest rate over short period is less as compared to when lending is made for a longer period of time, thus affecting the Revenue Efficiency.

The methodological framework highlighted that Technical Efficiency and allocative efficiency (output oriented) comprise of Revenue Efficiency. Table: 5 indicates that allocative inefficiency has always been higher than technical inefficiency. Thus the dominant source of revenue inefficiency is allocative inefficiency. The higher allocative inefficiency comparative to technical inefficiency implies that managers are not efficient in choosing the revenue maximizing mix of output given the output prices. Further, the Technical Efficiency components depict that all sector banks are operating at incorrect scale as depicted by low Scale Efficiency as compared to Pure Technical Efficiency. Scale inefficiency cautions that banks are not operating on the optimum scale. They need to expand their business not only by opening new branches, but also by increasing their customer base by indulging in quality of services and effective customer relation management to achieve economies of scale.

Cost Efficiency vis-à-vis Revenue Efficiency of Scheduled Commercial Banks in India Across Ownership

Thus, specifically considering points of time, Public Sector Banks have higher Cost Efficiency score in 2000-01, Private Sector Banks in 2004-05 while Foreign Sector Banks in 2008-09, 2012-13 and 2016-17. Similarly, on the revenue side, Public Sector Banks have higher Revenue Efficiency scores in 2000-01 and 2004-05, Foreign Sector Banks in 2008-09 and 2016-17 and Private Sector Banks in 2012-13.

Holistically, the efficiency score across ownership highlights that Public Sector Banks have the highest level of inefficiency on the cost side as compared to private sector and Foreign Sector Banks. Disguised employment has been major troubling factor for PSBs. It leads to hiked salary bills with negligible productivity (Bhatia and Mahendru, 2015). PSBs are also not able to utilise their capital investment effectively (Jagannathan, 2014). In meeting their social objectives they open their branches in the rural areas. But this investment does not pay back itself as the customer is comparatively less literate and lesser tech-savvy. This makes them cost inefficient. However, relative to Cost Efficiency, Revenue Efficiency scores of PSBs are better. Public Sector Banks have long and old existence. They also have large number of branches extended all over the country. They are deeply protected by the Government of India which holds 51% share in their share holding. Most importantly, the customers have trust and confidence on these banks. This helps them to earn better revenues. Private Sector Banks seem to be better on the revenue side at most of points of time. Private Sector Banks have been the pioneers in offering services through Electronic Banking, Mobile Banking, Credit Card, Electronic Fund Transfers (EFTs), Real Time Gross Settlement (RTGs) and National Electronic Fund Transfer (NEFTs) etc. This reduces their normal functioning cost in the long run. Moreover, they seem to have recognised the significance of issues relating to Service Quality Management and Total Quality Management. They provide prompt and quality services to the customers. This all led to improved Revenue Efficiency of Private Sector Banks. Foreign Sector Banks show more inefficiency on the revenue side as these have higher Cost Efficiency score in comparison to Revenue Efficiency scores. Foreign Sector Banks save their infrastructural cost as they do not exist in brick and mortar and follow virtual banking. They save on the cost of advertising their products and services as their focus is on corporate clients and they do not compete for the share of retail clientage.

Robustness Test Across Ownership

After examining the results derived from DEA, the issue of attention at this moment is whether the difference in the Revenue Efficiency and Cost Efficiency is statistically significant for Public, Private and Foreign Sector Banks at different points of time. For checking the same, Analysis of Variances (ANOVA) is applied. The test is applied with the hypothesis that there is no difference in Revenue Efficiency and Cost Efficiency and their other components of Public, Private and Foreign Sector Banks. The results of ANOVA are given in the Table: 6 below:

Table: 6 Results of ANOVA for all Efficiency Scores

Efficiency Year	Cost Efficiency				Revenue Efficiency			
	Banks	Mean Scores	F test	Sig.	Banks	Mean Scores	F test	Sig.
2000-01	Public Sector Banks	0.578	1.709	.187	Public Sector Banks	0.749	3.456**	.036
	Private Sector Banks	0.496			Private Sector Banks	0.625		
	Foreign Sector Banks	0.569			Foreign Sector Banks	0.702		
2004-05	Public Sector Banks	0.684	0.187	.830	Public Sector Banks	0.732	2.378	.099
	Private Sector Banks	0.702			Private Sector Banks	0.626		
	Foreign Sector Banks	0.668			Foreign Sector Banks	0.615		
2008-09	Public Sector Banks	0.650	8.361*	.001	Public Sector Banks	0.681	1.526	.225
	Private Sector Banks	0.698			Private Sector Banks	0.743		
	Foreign Sector Banks	0.808			Foreign Sector Banks	0.754		
2012-13	Public Sector Banks	0.368	22.160*	.000	Public Sector Banks	0.518	1.976	.146
	Private Sector Banks	0.431			Private Sector Banks	0.624		
	Foreign Sector Banks	0.642			Foreign Sector Banks	0.585		
2016-17	Public Sector Banks	0.401	15.962*	.000	Public Sector Banks	0.552	36.063	.000
	Private Sector Banks	0.397			Private Sector Banks	0.408		
	Foreign Sector Banks	0.634			Foreign Sector Banks	0.685		

*, **Significant at 1% and 5% level of Significance respectively

Table: 6 shows the robustness test. The results of ANOVA reveal that there exists a statistically significant difference among different sector banks in case of Cost Efficiency in the year 2008-09, 2012-13 and 2016-17. As Cost Efficiency has F value of 8.361, 22.160 and 15.962 in 2008-09, 2012-13 and 2016-17 respectively and are statistically significant at 1% level of significance. Revenue Efficiency has F score of 3.456 and 36.063 in the year 2000-01 and 2016-17, which means that the difference is significant at 5% and 1% level of significance respectively. Further, the results show that the difference among groups in case of Cost Efficiency and Revenue Efficiency scores is statistically insignificant for the rest of the years.

Overall, the results of ANOVA depict that cost and Revenue Efficiency score are different for Public Sector Banks, Private Sector Banks and Foreign Sector Banks at some point of time. In order to further check as to between which groups of banks the difference is significant, Post Hoc test was applied. Table: 7 shows the Multiple Comparisons Post Hoc Test- Tukey HSD.

Table: 7 Multiple Comparisons Post Hoc Test - Tukey HSD

Years	Efficiency	Cost Efficiency				Revenue Efficiency			
		(I) Banks	(J) Banks	Mean Difference (I-J)	Std. Error	(I) Banks	(J) Banks	Mean Difference (I-J)	Std. Error
2000-01		Public Sector Banks	Private Sector Banks	0.08155	0.05011	Public Sector Banks	Private Sector Banks	0.1234**	0.04787
			Foreign Sector Banks	0.00844	0.04819		Foreign Sector Banks	0.04616	0.04603
		Private Sector Banks	Public Sector Banks	-0.08155	0.05011	Private Sector Banks	Public Sector Banks	-0.1234**	0.04787
			Foreign Sector Banks	-0.07311	0.04635		Foreign Sector Banks	-0.07724	0.04428
		Foreign Sector Banks	Public Sector Banks	-0.00844	0.04819	Foreign Sector Banks	Public Sector Banks	-0.04616	0.04603
			Private Sector Banks	0.07311	0.04635		Private Sector Banks	0.07724	0.04428
2004-05		Public Sector Banks	Private Sector Banks	-0.01774	0.05537	Public Sector Banks	Private Sector Banks	0.1167	0.0582
			Foreign Sector Banks	0.0167	0.05692		Foreign Sector Banks	-0.10551	0.05983
		Private Sector Banks	Public Sector Banks	0.01774	0.05537	Private Sector Banks	Public Sector Banks	-0.1167	0.0582
			Foreign Sector Banks	0.03444	0.05645		Foreign Sector Banks	-0.01118	0.05933
		Foreign Sector Banks	Public Sector Banks	-0.0167	0.05692	Foreign Sector Banks	Public Sector Banks	0.10551	0.05983
			Private Sector Banks	-0.03444	0.05645		Private Sector Banks	0.01118	0.05933
2008-09		Public Sector Banks	Private Sector Banks	-0.04835	0.03974	Public Sector Banks	Private Sector Banks	-0.06209	0.04666
			Foreign Sector Banks	-0.15862*	0.0392		Foreign Sector Banks	-0.07342	0.04602
		Private Sector Banks	Public Sector Banks	0.04835	0.03974	Private Sector Banks	Public Sector Banks	0.06209	0.04666
			Foreign Sector Banks	-0.11028**	0.04209		Foreign Sector Banks	-0.01133	0.04941
		Foreign Sector Banks	Public Sector Banks	0.15862*	0.0392	Foreign Sector Banks	Public Sector Banks	0.07342	0.04602
			Private Sector Banks	0.11028**	0.04209		Private Sector Banks	0.01133	0.04941
2012-13		Public Sector Banks	Private Sector Banks	-0.27361*	0.04307	Public Sector Banks	Private Sector Banks	-0.10558	0.05478
			Foreign Sector Banks	-0.06329	0.0478		Foreign Sector Banks	-0.06694	0.04935
		Private Sector Banks	Public Sector Banks	0.27361*	0.04307	Private Sector Banks	Public Sector Banks	0.10558	0.05478
			Foreign Sector Banks	0.21032*	0.0464		Foreign Sector Banks	0.03863	0.05317
		Foreign Sector Banks	Public Sector Banks	0.06329	0.0478	Foreign Sector Banks	Public Sector Banks	0.06694	0.04935
			Private Sector Banks	-0.21032*	0.0464		Private Sector Banks	-0.03863	0.05317
2016-17		Public Sector Banks	Private Sector Banks	-0.00585	0.5881	Public Sector Banks	Private Sector Banks	-0.13221**	0.03045
			Foreign Sector Banks	-.24204**	0.4963		Foreign Sector Banks	0.14402**	0.03609
		Private Sector Banks	Public Sector Banks	0.00585	0.5881	Private Sector Banks	Public Sector Banks	0.13221**	0.03045
			Foreign Sector Banks	-0.23620**	0.5381		Foreign Sector Banks	0.27623**	0.03302
		Foreign Sector Banks	Public Sector Banks	0.24204**	0.4963	Foreign Sector Banks	Public Sector Banks	-0.14402**	0.03609
			Private Sector Banks	0.23620**	0.5381		Private Sector Banks	-0.27623**	0.03302

*, **Significant at 1% and 5% level of Significance respectively

The Tukey Post Hoc test reveals that mean difference between foreign-public and foreign-private is statistically significant for Cost Efficiency in the year 2008-09, 2012-13 and 2016-17. The mean difference between foreign-public is 0.15862 and between foreign-private is 0.11028 and is statistically significant at 1% and 5% level of significance respectively. In addition, the mean difference in Cost Efficiency in 2012-13 between foreign-public (0.27361) and foreign-private (0.21032) and are statistically significant at 1% level of significance. The mean difference between foreign-public is 0.24204 and between foreign-private is 0.23620 and both are statistically significant at 5% level of significance.

Basically, FSBs have professional work culture and business philosophy. Moreover, they are mainly operating in metro cities where people are more tech-savvy. FSBs are able to recover their operating cost which they have incurred on e-resources. Moreover, they mainly focus on corporate clients and do not compete for the share of retail clientage. This reduces their promotion and advertising cost as well. On the other hand, Revenue Efficiency scores depict that the mean difference between Public-Private is 0.1234, with p value of 0.013 which was significant at 5% level of significance in 2000-01. The mean difference between foreign-public is 0.13221 and between foreign-private is 0.27623 and both are statistically significant at 5% level of significance. PSBs have old existence and reputable position in the market, their being the Government protected banks, helps them to earn greater revenues. Moreover, PSBs with the introduction of reforms and competition in the market extended their business to fee based services like letter of credit, bank guarantee, factoring, underwriting and custodial services etc. The cumulative effect of all these efforts seemed to have accelerated their revenue efficiency in the year 2000-01.

Conclusion

Scheduled Commercial Banks are not able to maintain their input-output synchronization in terms of cost and revenue. There exists a room for improvement for SCBs. Bank managers need to establish equilibrium between inputs and outputs of banks keeping in mind their prices in the country's dynamic environment. The results of the study indicate that Foreign Sector Banks are most Cost Efficient Banks in the recent time period i.e. 2008-09 and 2012-13. No doubt, banks operating in different sectors are regulated and fully controlled by Reserve Bank of India; still, there are some differences among them in terms of their working, customer base, employee base, spread of their branches and working environment etc. Like, Foreign Sector Banks have disciplined work environment and employ trained and specialised staff with the main focus on corporate clients. On the other hand, both domestic banks i.e. Public Sector and Private Sector banks operate in the rural, urban and semi-urban areas.

Certainly, PSBs and Private Sector Banks have similar norms, but their existence, goals and interference from Government builds a gap among them. Public Sector Banks have the obligation to fulfil social objectives along with achieving profit whereas Private Sector Banks focus mainly on the profit maximisation objective. Thus, there is a need that banks operating in different sectors to be more professional. Private Sector Banks and Foreign Sector Banks too must equally share society oriented targets with Public Sector Banks so that social responsibilities along with revenues is evenly divided. Reserve Bank of India is making efforts towards this end. It has revamped the priority sector lending norms according to which Foreign Sector Banks with more than 20 branches too have to move towards 40% Total Priority Sector Target by 2018 while FSBs with less than 20 branches have to attain this target by 2019-20. Thus it is hoped that the gap between the banks operating under divergent ownership would be reduced in the near future and Indian banking sector as a whole would become more efficient.

The present study has made an effort to consider a major research gap by simultaneously evaluating the Cost and Revenue Efficiency scores of Indian Scheduled Commercial Banksat essential points of times.

The research can further be extended by studying the efficiency of banks over several years. A comparison of efficiency scores in reformatory and post reformatory time period or the crisis time period too can be made. Besides, various bank specific, industry specific and economy specific factors too can be considered for determining their impact on Cost and Revenue Efficiency of banks.

References

Ahmed, T. (2008). *Efficiency analysis of commercial banks in Pakistan* (Doctoral Dissertation). University of Agriculture, Faisalabad, Pakistan.

Ariff, M., & Can, L. (2008). Cost and profit efficiency of Chinese banks: A non-parametric analysis. *China Economic Review, 19*(2), 260-273.

Bader, M. K. I., Mohamad, S., Ariff, M., & Hassan, T. (2008). Cost, revenue and profit efficiency of Islamic versus conventional banks: International evidence using Data Envelopment Analysis. *Islamic Economic Studies, 15*(2), 23-76.

Benston, G. J. (1965). Branch banking and economies of scale. *The Journal of Finance, 20*(2), 312-331.

Berger, A. N., & Humphrey, D. (1997). Efficiency of Financial Institutions: International survey and directions for future research. *European Journal of Operational Research, 98*(2), 175-212.

Berger, A. N., &Mester, L. J. (2003). Explaining the dramatic changes in performance of US banks: Technological change, deregulation, and dynamic changes in competition. *Journal of Financial Intermediation, 12*(1), 57–95.

Berger, A. N., Hunter, W. C., &Timme, S. G. (1993). The efficiency of financial institutions: A review and preview of research past, present and future. *Journal of Banking and Finance, 17*(2 and 3), 221–250.

Bhatia, A., & Mahendru, M. (2015). Assessment of technical efficiency of public sector banks in India using data envelopment analysis. *Eurasian Journal of Business and Economics, 8*(15), 115-140.

Burki, A. A., &Niazi, G. S. K. (2006). Impact of financial reforms on efficiency of state-owned, private and foreign banks in Pakistan (CMER Working Paper No. 06-49). Retrieved from http://saber.eaber.org/sites/default/files/documents/ LUMS_Burki_2006.pdf

Cetorelli, N., &Gambera, M. (2001). Banking market structure, financial dependence and growth: International evidence from industry data. *The Journal of Finance, 56*(2), 617–648.

Chatterjee, S., Das, P., & Gupta, A. (2014). The anatomy of profitability, efficiency and productivity of regional rural banks in selected backward districts of West Bengal: A panel data investigation, *Vidyasagar University Journal of Commerce, 19*, 34-58.

Das, A., Nag, A., & Ray, S. C. (2005). Liberalisation, ownership and efficiency in Indian banking: A non-parametric analysis. *Economic and Political Weekly, 40*(12), 1190-1197.

Egesa, K. (2010). *Financial Sector Liberalization and Productivity Change in Ugandas Commercial Banking Sector. The African Economic Research Consortium, Nairobi, Kenya. Retrieved from http://dspace.africaportal.org/jspui/bitstream/ 123456789/32145/1/RP202.pdf?1*

Girardone, C., Molyneux, P., & Gardener, E. P. (2004). Analysing the determinants of bank efficiency: The case of Italian banks. *Applied Economics, 36*(3), 215-227.

Gulati, R. (2011a). *Evaluation of technical, pure technical and scale efficiencies of Indian banks: An analysis from cross-sectional perspective.* Paper presented in 13th Annual Conference on Money and Finance in the Indian Economy, Indira Gandhi Institute of Development Research, Mumbai. Retrieved fromhttp://igidr.ac.in/conf/money/mfc-13/Evaluation%20of%20technical,%20pure%20technical%20and%20scale%20efficiencies%20of%20Indian%20Banks.pdf

Gulati, R. (2011b). *Efficiency in Indian commercial banks: A post-deregulation experience*, (Doctoral Dissertation). Guru Nanak Dev University, Amritsar, India.

Gulati, R., & Kumar, S. (2011). Impact of non-traditional activities on the efficiency of Indian banks: an empirical investigation. *Macroeconomics and Finance in Emerging Market Economies (An international journal of Routledge, Taylor & Francis Group), 4*(1), p125-166.

Jagannathan, R. (2014, December 30). Re: 3 Modi matters for PSU banks: Less capital, more autonomy, productive staff. [Web log comment].Retrieved form

Jain, S. (2011, November 30). Re: India's private or public sector banks: Who is better? [Web log comment]. Retrieved from http://www.mbaskool.com/business -articles/finance/1061-indias-private-or-public-sector-banks-who-is-better.html

Kamarudin, F., Nordin, B. A. A., Muhammad, J., & Hamid, M. A. A. (2014). Cost, revenue and profit efficiency of Islamic and conventional banking sector: Empirical evidence from Gulf cooperative council countries. *Global Business Review, 15*(1), 1-24.

Kumar, P. (2006). *Banking Sector Efficiency in Globalized Economy*. New Delhi: Deep and Deep Publications Pvt. Ltd.

Kumar, S. (2013). Banking reforms and the evolution of cost efficiency in Indian public sector banks. *Economic Change and Restructuring, 46*(2), 143-182.

Levin, R. (1997). Financial development and economic growth: Views and agenda. *Journal of Economic Literature, 35*(2), 688–726.

Liem, V. T., &Hien, N. N. (2020). Exploring the impact of dynamic environment and CEO's psychology characteristics on using management accounting system. *Cogent Business & Management, 7*(1), 1712768.

Loukoianova, E. (2008). *Analysis of the efficiency and profitability of the Japanese banking system* (IMF Working Papers), Retrieved from http://ssrn.com/ abstract=1112205

Lovell, C. A. K. (1993). Production frontier and productive efficiency. In H O Fried, C A K Lovell and S S Schmidt (Eds.), *The measurement of productive efficiency –Techniques and applications*, London: Oxford University Press.

Niazi, G. (2003). *Measuringcost efficiency and productivity change of commercial banks in Pakistan*, 1991-2000(Doctoral Dissertation). Quaid-I-Azam University, Islamabad, Pakistan.

Pančurová, D., &Lyócsa, S. (2013). Determinants of commercial banks' efficiency: Evidence from 11 CEE countries. *Finance a Uver, 63*(2), 152-179.

Pasiouras, F., &Kosmidou, K. (2007). Factors influencing the profitability of domestic and foreign commercial banks in the European Union. *Research in International Business and Finance, 21*(2), 222-237.

Portela, M. C. A. S., &Thanassoulis, E. (2007). Developing a decomposable measure of profit efficiency using DEA. *Journal of the Operational Research Society, 58*(4), 481-490.

Raina, D., & Sharma, S. K. (2013). Determinants of cost efficiency of commercial banks in India: DEA Evidence. *IUP Journal of Bank Management, 12*(2), 17-30.

Rajan, R.G., & Zingales, L. (1995). What do we know about capital structure? Some evidence from international data, *Journal of Finance, 50*(5), 1421-1460.

Ram Mohan, T. T., & Ray, S. C. (2004). Comparing performance of public and private sector banks: A revenue maximisation efficiency approach. *Economic and Political Weekly, 39*(12), 1271-1276.

Reserve Bank of India (2000-01). *Report on trend and progress of banking in India*, Mumbai: Jayant Printers.

Reserve Bank of India (2003-04). *Report on trend and progress of banking in India*, Mumbai: Jayant Printers.

Reserve Bank of India (2004-05). *Report on trend and progress of banking in India*, Mumbai: Jayant Printers.

Reserve Bank of India (2008-09). *Report on trend and progress of banking in India*, Mumbai: Jayant Printers.

Reserve Bank of India (2012-13). *Report on trend and progress of banking in India*, Mumbai: Jayant Printers.

Reserve Bank of India (2016-17). *Report on trend and progress of banking in India*, Mumbai: Jayant Printers.

Sahoo, B. K., Sengupta, J., & Mandal, A. (2007). Productive performance evaluation of the banking sector in India using data envelopment analysis. *International Journal of Operations Research,* 4 (2), 63-79.

Sufian, F. (2009). Determinants of bank efficiency during unstable macroeconomic environment: Empirical evidence from Malaysia. *Research in International Business and Finance, 23*(1), 54-77.

Tandon, A., Jeremy A. L., David B. E., & Christopher J. L. M. (2003). Health System Efficiency: Concepts, In Christopher J.L. Murray and David B. Evans (Eds.). *Health Systems Performance Assessment: Debates, Methods and Empiricism* (pp. 683-691). Switzerland: World Health Organization.

Uddin, S. S., & Suzuki, Y. (2011). Financial reform, ownership and performance in banking industry: The case of Bangladesh. *International Journal of Business and Management, 6*(7), 28-39.

Valverde, S. C., Humphrey, D. B., &Fernández, F. R. (2003). Bank deregulation is better than mergers. *Journal of International Financial Markets, Institutions and Money, 13*(5), 429-449.

Wanniarachchige, M. K., & Suzuki, Y. (2011). *Performance dynamics of Indian commercial banks: Does ownership matter?* Paper presented at the 2011 Maui International Academic Conference, Maui, Hawaii, USA.

Dr.Aparna Bhatia, Assistant Professor, University School of Financial Studies, Guru Nanak Dev University Amritsar. She can be reached at aparnamohindru@yahoo.co.in

Dr. Megha Mahendruis working as an Assistant Professor in the Department of Commerce and Business Administration, Khalsa College, Amritsar. She can be reached at mahendru.megha30@gmail.com

Submission Guidelines

NMIMS Management Review invites original research papers (both qualitative and quantitative) for publication in the journal. The research papers can be based on academic as well as industry practices. However we will not publish any cases studies, book reviews in the current format of the journal.

The journal receives good amount of research papers for which we have a high rejection rate. So the authors should be careful to avoid any mistakes that may lead to rejection of the research paper.

1. Email Id: Please submit all research papers to the following email id: managingeditor@sbm.nmims.edu
2. Please don't mark your mail to any personal email id. You will receive all communication from this email id.
3. Submission Platform: At this point of time, we are using email for submission, review and communication, However, in future we may move to an online platform. We will announce here as well as write mail to authors/ reviewers
4. Format: All articles including abstract should be typed in MSWord format, 12 Pt font sizes, double spaced in California FB. All Tables, Figures and Charts should be taken to the end of the article. The author can mention 'Table-1 here/Figure-1 here/Chart-1 here inside the text). Please note all titles to tables, figures and charts should be numbered and mentioned BELOW the table. Please note we do not receive any research paper in any other format including PDF.
5. Abstract: Each research paper should be accompanied by an abstract of 150-200 words. Notes should be numbered serially and presented at the end of the article. Note should contain more than a mere reference. The abstract should have headers in sequence as Purpose, Design/Methodology/ Approach; Findings, Practical Implications and Originality/Value

   - Contributor's Affiliation: The contributor should provide her/his affiliation in the first page only. The author details IS NOT TO BE mentioned anywhere in the main article. The first page of the article should cover the following
   - Title of the Paper in 14 pt, 1.5 spacing on California FB.
   - Name of the Author in 12 Pt, 1.5 spacing on California FB.
   - Affiliation of the author, Email address and mobile number should be mentioned below the name in 12 Pt, 1.5 spacing on California FB.
   - Complete Postal address should be mentioned below the affiliation.
   - Spelling: Please use 'z' in '-ize' and '-ization' words. We receive manuscripts only in British English.
   - Quotations: Use single quotes. For quotations within quotations, use double quotes. Spellings of words in quotations should not be changed. Quotations of 45 words or more should be set apart by indenting the quotation (and adding a line space above and below).
   - Numbers: Use 'nineteenth century', '1980s'. Spell out numbers from one to nine; 10 and above to remain in figures. However, for exact measurements use only figures (3 km; 9 per cent). Use 'per cent' in text and '%' in tables and figures. Use thousands and millions, not lakhs and crores.
   - Italics: Use of italics and diacriticals should be minimized but consistent.
   - Tables and figures: Should be indicated by number separately ('Table 1'), not by placement ('Table below'). Present each table and figure on a separate sheet of paper, gathering them together at the end

6. References: A consolidated alphabetical list of all books, articles, essays and theses referred to (including any referred to in the tables, graphs and maps) should be provided. It should be typed in double-spacing and will be printed at the end of the article. All articles, books, and theses should be listed in alphabetical order of author, giving the author's surname first, followed by initials. If more than one publication by the same author is listed, the items should be given in chronological order. References should be embedded in text in the anthropological style. For example, '(Panda; 2020)'. Citations should be first alphabetical and then chronological. For example, '(Ajay 2019; Sumit1997; Wright 1960)'. Citations and References should adhere to the guidelines below (based on the Publication Manual of the American Psychological Association, 6th edition). Some examples are given below:
(a) In text citations:
One work by one author: (Kessler, 2003, p. 50) or 'Kessler (2003) found that among the epidemiological samples..'.
One work by two authors: (Joreskog&Sorborn, 2007, pp. 50–66) or Joreskog and Sorborn (2007) found that..
One work by three or more authors: (Basu, Banerji& Chatterjee, 2007) [first instance]; Basu et al. (2007) [Second instance onwards].

Groups or organizations or universities: (University of Pittsburgh, 2007) or University of Pittsburgh (2007).
Authors with same surname: Include the initials in all the in-text citations even if the year of publication differs, e.g., (I. Light, 2006; M.A. Light, 2008).
Works with no identified author or anonymous author: Cite the first few words of the reference entry (title) and then the year, e.g., ('Study finds', 2007); (Anonymous, 1998).

If abbreviations are provided, then the style to be followed is: (National Institute of Mental Health [NIMH], 2003) in the first citation and (NIMH, 2003) in subsequent citations.
Two or more works by same author: (Gogel, 1990, 2006, in press)
Two or more works with different authors: (Gogel, 1996; Miller, 1999)
Secondary sources: Allport's diary (as cited in Nicholson, 2003).

(b) Books:
Patnaik, Utsa (2007). The republic of hunger. New Delhi: Three Essays Collective.

(c) Edited Books:
Amanor, Kojo S., &Moyo, S. (Eds) (2008). Land and sustainable development in Africa. London and New York: Zed Books.

(d) Translated books:
Amin, S. (1976). Unequal development (trans. B. Pearce). London and New York: Monthly Review Press.

(e) Book chapters:
Chachra, S. (2011). The national question in India. In S. Moyo and P. Yeros (Eds), Reclaiming the nation. (pp. 67–78). London and New York: Pluto Press.

(f) Journal articles:
Foster, J.B. (2010). The financialization of accumulation. Monthly Review, 62(5), 1-17. doi: 10.1037/0278-6133.24.2.225 [Doi number optional]

(g) Newsletter article, no author:
Six sites meet for comprehensive anti-gang intiative conference. (2006, November/December). OOJDP News @ a Glance. Retrievd from http://www.ncrjs.gov/html

(h) Newspaper article:
Schwartz, J. (1993, September 30). Obesity affects economic, social status. The Washington Post, pp. A1, A4.

(i) In-press article:
Briscoe, R. (in press). Egocentric spatial representation in action and perception.Philosophy and Phenomenological Research. Retrieved from http://cogprints.org/5780/1/ECSRAP.F07.pdf

(j) Non-English reference book, title translated into English:
Real Academia Espanola. (2001). Diccionario de la lenguaespanola [Dictionary of the Spanish Language] (22nd ed.). Madrid, Spain: Author.

(k) Special issue or section in a journal:
Haney, C., & Wiener, R.L. (Eds) (2004). Capital punishment in the United States [Special Issue]. Psychology, Public Policy, and Law, 10(4), 1-17.

7. Publication Ethics: NMIMS Management Review is committed to upholding the integrity of the academic record. The journal encourages authors to refer to the Committee on Publication Ethics' International Standards for Authors and view the Publication Ethics page on the journal website.

8. Copyright: Authors will be provided with a copyright form once the research paper is accepted for publication. The submission will be considered as final only after the filled-in and signed copyright form is received. In case there are two or more authors, the corresponding author needs to sign the copyright form.

8(a). All photographs and scanned images should have a resolution of minimum 300 dpi/1500 pixels and their format should be TIFF or JPEG. Due permissions should be taken for copyright protected photographs/images. Even for photographs/images available in the public domain, it should be clearly ascertained whether or not their reproduction requires permission for purposes of publishing (which is a profit-making endeavour). All photographs/scanned images should be provided separately.

www.ingramcontent.com/pod-product-compliance
Lightning Source LLC
LaVergne TN
LVHW081544060526
838200LV00048B/2207